THE

HISTORY OF

THE NFL

BY JAMES BREN

CHAPTERS

INTRODUCTION

Football is more than just a game in America. It is a cultural phenomenon, a way of life, and a symbol of American identity. And at the center of this football craze is the National Football League (NFL), the premier professional football league in the world.

"The History of the NFL" is a comprehensive look at the league's storied past, from its humble beginnings to its current status as a global entertainment behemoth. This book takes readers on a journey through the NFL's early days, when it was little more than a ragtag group of teams playing in dusty stadiums for small crowds.

Through the decades, the NFL has grown in size and stature, attracting more fans, more talent, and more money. Along the way, the league has faced numerous challenges, from labor disputes to changing cultural attitudes towards violence in sports.

This book delves into the personalities and rivalries that have defined the league over the years, from the iconic players like Bronko Nagurski, Jim Brown, Joe Montana, and Tom Brady, to the colorful coaches like Vince Lombardi, Bill Walsh, and Bill Belichick.

It also examines the impact of the NFL on American culture and society, from its role in promoting civil rights to its influence on popular culture, fashion, and even politics.

"The History of the NFL" is a must-read for any fan of the game or anyone interested in the evolution of American culture and society over the last century. This book is a tribute to the people, moments, and events that have made the NFL such an important and enduring part of American life.

THE FOUNDERS

The NFL is one of the most popular and lucrative sports leagues in the world. But like all great institutions, it had humble beginnings. The NFL was founded on August 20, 1920, in Canton, Ohio, by a group of ten men who saw the potential for professional football to become a popular and profitable sport.

These ten men were:

1. Jim Thorpe - Arguably the greatest athlete of the 20th century, Thorpe was a Native American who excelled in multiple sports, including football, baseball, and track and field. Thorpe played for several professional football teams before helping to found the NFL. He served as the league's first president and helped establish many of the rules and regulations that still govern the game today.

2. George Halas - Known as the "father of the NFL," Halas was a player, coach, and owner who spent his entire career with the Chicago Bears. Halas helped to establish the NFL as a major professional sports league and was a key figure in the development of the league's television and marketing strategies.

3. Ralph Hay - Hay was the owner of the Canton Bulldogs, one of the top professional football teams in the country at the time of the NFL's founding. Hay hosted the meeting in Canton where the NFL was established and served as the league's first secretary.

4. Frank Nied - Nied was a sports writer who helped promote professional football in the early 20th century. He was one of the driving forces behind the establishment of the NFL and helped to draft the league's first constitution.

5. Carl Storck - Storck was the owner of the Dayton Triangles, one of the oldest professional football teams in the country. He played a key role in the formation of the NFL and served as the league's first treasurer.

6. Joseph Carr - Carr was a sports promoter who helped to establish the NFL as a major professional sports league. He served as the league's president from 1921 to 1939 and was instrumental in developing the league's structure, including the establishment of the first championship game in 1933.

7. Leo Lyons - Lyons was the owner of the Rochester Jeffersons, one of the original professional football teams in the country. He played a key role in the establishment of the NFL and served as the league's vice president from 1920 to 1921.

8. Chris O'Brien - O'Brien was the owner of the Milwaukee Badgers, one of the top professional football teams in the country at the time of the NFL's founding. He helped to establish the league and served as the NFL's treasurer from 1921 to 1939.

9. Bert Bell - Bell was a player, coach, and owner who spent his career with the Philadelphia Eagles. He helped to establish the NFL as a major professional sports league and served as the league's commissioner from 1946 to 1959.

10. Tim Mara - Mara was the owner of the New York Giants, one of the most successful professional football teams in the country. He played a key role in the establishment of the NFL and served as the league's treasurer from 1939 to 1959.

These ten men were the founders of the NFL, but they were far from the only ones who helped to shape the league in its early years. Over the next few decades, the NFL would continue to grow and evolve, with new owners, players, and coaches joining the ranks and contributing to the league's success.

THE 1920'S

1920

The year was 1920, and the United States was experiencing a period of great change and upheaval. The end of World War I had brought about a new era of prosperity and optimism, and many Americans were eager to embrace new forms of entertainment and leisure. It was in this context that the NFL was founded.

The NFL's origins can be traced back to a meeting that took place on August 20, 1920, in Canton, Ohio. The meeting was attended by representatives from ten different professional football teams, including the Akron Pros, Canton Bulldogs, and Cleveland Tigers. The purpose of the meeting was to establish a governing body for professional football and to create a structure for organizing and scheduling games.

The founding members of the NFL were a diverse group of individuals, including team owners, coaches, and former players. They were united by a common goal: to establish professional football as a legitimate and popular sport in the United States. At the time, professional football was still a relatively new and untested concept, and there was little public interest or financial support for the sport.

In its early years, the NFL was a loose and informal organization. There were no set rules or regulations, and teams were free to schedule games and compete against one another as they saw fit. This lack of structure and organization presented significant challenges for the league, as it made it difficult to attract fans and generate revenue.

One of the biggest challenges facing the NFL in its early years was the lack of a championship game. Without a clear and definitive way to determine the best team in the league, there was little incentive for fans to follow the sport or for teams to invest in their players and infrastructure. To address this issue, the NFL established a playoff system in 1922, culminating in a championship game between the top two teams in the league.

The early years of the NFL were also marked by a great deal of uncertainty and instability. Teams frequently folded or merged with other teams, and the league struggled to maintain a consistent and stable roster of franchises. This instability was exacerbated by the fact that the NFL was still a relatively minor sport at the time, with little media coverage or public attention.

Despite these challenges, the NFL managed to survive and grow in its early years. The league's founding members were committed to the sport and to establishing professional football as a viable and legitimate form of entertainment. They worked tirelessly to promote the league and to attract new fans and investors.

In conclusion, the year 1920 was a pivotal moment in the history of American sports. The founding of the NFL represented a bold and visionary move by a group of individuals who saw the potential for professional football to become a major force in American sports and entertainment. Although the league faced significant challenges in its early years, the commitment and dedication of its founding members helped to establish a foundation for the future success and growth of the sport.

1921

The NFL was founded on August 20, 1920, and its first season was played the following year in 1921. The league started off with only ten teams, most of which were located in the Midwest, and quickly gained popularity. The 1921 season was an important year for the NFL, as it established many of the foundational elements that the league still uses today.

The Teams

The ten teams that made up the NFL in 1921 were the Akron Pros, Buffalo All-Americans, Canton Bulldogs, Chicago Cardinals, Chicago Staleys (later renamed the Chicago Bears), Cleveland Indians, Dayton Triangles, Decatur Staleys (later renamed the Chicago Bears), Rochester Jeffersons, and Rock Island Independents. Many of these teams had been around for several years, but the NFL brought them together under one league.

The Rules

The rules of the NFL in 1921 were similar to today's rules, but there were some notable differences. For example, the field was 110 yards long instead of the current 100 yards. Also, the forward pass was still a relatively new concept in football, and it was not as common as it is today. Players were not required to wear helmets until the 1940s, and many of the protective measures that are standard in today's game were not yet in place.

The Schedule

The 1921 NFL season was shorter than the current season, with each team playing only 11 games. There were no playoffs or Super Bowl at this time; the team with the best regular-season record was declared the league champion.

The Akron Pros finished the season with an 8-0-3 record, giving them the title of NFL champions for 1921.

The Players

The players in the NFL in 1921 were mostly white, and many of them were also college students. The pay was not great, and most players held other jobs during the off-season. Some of the notable players from this era include Jim Thorpe, who played for the Canton Bulldogs, and Red Grange, who would not join the NFL until 1925.

Impact

The NFL in 1921 was still in its infancy, but it was already making an impact on American sports culture. Football was becoming a popular spectator sport, and the NFL was leading the way in organizing and promoting the game. The league was also laying the groundwork for future expansion and growth, which would eventually lead to the NFL becoming the most popular sports league in the United States.

The 1921 NFL season was an important year for the league, as it established many of the foundational elements that still define the league today. From the ten teams that made up the league to the rules of the game, the 1921 season set the stage for the NFL's future success. Despite its humble beginnings, the NFL would go on to become a cultural icon and a multi-billion dollar industry.

1922: A Year of Expansion and Turmoil

The year 1922 was a significant year for the NFL, as it marked the start of a period of expansion and turmoil. The NFL, which had been formed in 1920, was still a relatively young organization, with only a handful of teams scattered across the Midwest. However, in 1922, the league underwent significant changes that would shape its future.

Expansion

One of the most significant changes to the NFL in 1922 was the addition of several new teams. The league expanded from ten teams in 1921 to twenty teams in 1922, as teams from smaller leagues, such as the Ohio League and the New York Pro Football League, were absorbed into the NFL. This expansion brought in new markets and fan bases, helping to grow the popularity of professional football across the country.

However, this expansion was not without its challenges. The NFL was still a relatively disorganized and decentralized organization, and the addition of new teams only exacerbated these issues. Many of the new teams were poorly managed, with little regard for the rules and regulations of the league. This led to a number of disputes and controversies, as teams argued over player eligibility and scheduling conflicts.

Turmoil

The expansion of the NFL in 1922 also brought about a great deal of turmoil within the league. One of the most significant issues facing the NFL in 1922 was the question of player compensation. At the time, most players were not paid a salary, but rather received a share of the team's profits. This led to disputes between players and team owners, as players sought a greater share of the revenue.

Another major issue facing the NFL in 1922 was the lack of consistent rules and regulations. Each team had its own set of rules, which led to confusion and disagreements on the field. The NFL attempted to address this issue by creating a committee to establish standardized rules for the league, but this effort was met with resistance from some team owners.

Finally, the NFL faced significant challenges from outside the league. College football was still the dominant form of the sport in 1922, and many colleges and universities refused to play against professional teams. This limited the opportunities for the NFL to showcase its talent and gain new fans.

In conclusion, the year 1922 was a significant year for the NFL, as it marked the start of a period of expansion and turmoil. The addition of new teams brought in new markets and fans, helping to grow the popularity of professional football across the country. However, this expansion also brought about significant challenges, including disputes over player compensation, inconsistent rules and regulations, and competition from college football. These challenges would continue to shape the NFL in the years to come, as the league worked to establish itself as a legitimate and respected professional sports organization.

1923

The NFL continued to evolve in 1923, with changes in teams, rules, and players. The league was still relatively new, but it was starting to gain a foothold in American sports culture.

The Teams

The NFL remained at twelve teams in 1923, with the same ten teams from the previous season returning, along with two new teams. The new teams were the St. Louis All-Stars and the Cincinnati Celts, both located in the Midwest. The league was starting to expand geographically, which would eventually lead to the NFL becoming a national league.

The Rules

The rules of the NFL in 1923 saw some significant changes, including the introduction of the "fourth down" rule. Previously, teams had only three downs to gain 10 yards for a first down. The fourth down was added to give teams an extra opportunity to keep possession of the ball. The forward pass continued to gain popularity, and teams were using it more often.

The Schedule

The NFL schedule in 1923 increased from 16 games to 20 games, with each team playing ten games at home and ten games on the road. This change was made in response to the league's growing popularity and the desire to give fans more opportunities to see their favorite teams play. Despite the longer season, there were still no playoffs or championship game.

The Players

The players in the NFL in 1923 were similar to the previous year, with most players being white and many of them also college students. However, the league was starting to attract more talented players, including Benny Friedman, who had gained national attention for his outstanding college football career. Friedman would eventually sign with the Cleveland Bulldogs in 1927, becoming one of the biggest stars in the NFL.

Impact

The NFL in 1923 continued to grow and establish itself as a significant force in American sports culture. The addition of two new teams and a longer season showed the league's commitment to expansion and providing more opportunities for fans to see their favorite teams play. The changes in rules, such as the fourth down rule, helped to increase the level of competition and excitement in the league.

The 1923 NFL season was another important year for the league, as it continued to evolve and grow. From expanding the number of teams and increasing the number of games, to attracting more talented players and making changes to the rules, the NFL was laying the groundwork for its future success. Despite its relatively short history, the NFL was already becoming a major player in American sports culture, and it was clear that its best years were still ahead.

1924

The year 1924 was an important year for the NFL, as it marked the first year of the league's existence under that name. Prior to 1924, the league was known as the American Professional Football Association (APFA). The name change came about in an effort to emphasize the league's national scope and to distance itself from semi-professional and college football, which were seen as inferior in quality.

The NFL's inaugural season featured 18 teams from across the country, including the Akron Pros, Chicago Bears, Cleveland Bulldogs, and Green Bay Packers. The league's structure was still in its infancy, with teams playing anywhere from 9 to 13 games, and no set playoff format.

One of the standout teams in the 1924 season was the Chicago Bears, led by legendary player-coach George

Halas. The Bears finished the season with a record of 6 wins, 1 loss, and 4 ties, earning them a share of the league championship with the Cleveland Bulldogs. Halas was instrumental in establishing the NFL's dominance over other football leagues, and the Bears' success in 1924 helped cement the league's status as the premier professional football organization in the country.

Another notable team in the 1924 season was the Frankford Yellow Jackets, based in Philadelphia. Led by future Hall of Famers Guy Chamberlin and Walt Kiesling, the Yellow Jackets finished with a record of 11 wins, 2 losses, and 1 tie, earning them a spot in a postseason exhibition game against a team of all-stars from other NFL teams. The game, held on December 14, 1924, was dubbed the "Chicago Charities" game, and it was the first-ever NFL championship game.

The Yellow Jackets defeated the all-stars 20-7, and while the game was not officially recognized as the NFL championship at the time, it is now considered the precursor to the modern Super Bowl. The success of the Chicago Charities game helped pave the way for a more formalized playoff structure in future NFL seasons.

Off the field, the NFL was still struggling with issues of player safety and financial stability. In 1924, the league introduced a rule requiring players to wear helmets, but many players still opted to go without them. Additionally, several teams struggled to make ends meet, and the league as a whole was still far from being the lucrative business it would become in later decades.

Despite these challenges, the NFL was slowly gaining in popularity and establishing itself as a major force in American sports. The league's success in 1924 laid the groundwork for future growth and expansion, setting the stage for the NFL to become the powerhouse organization it is today.

1925

The year 1925 marked the second season of the NFL under its current name. While the league was still relatively young and small, with just 12 teams compared to the previous season's 18, it was growing in popularity and importance as a professional sports organization.

One of the standout teams in the 1925 season was the Chicago Cardinals, led by player-coach Paddy Driscoll. The Cardinals finished the season with a record of 11 wins, 2 losses, and 1 tie, earning them the league championship. Driscoll was a key player for the team, leading them in both passing and rushing yards, as well as scoring 7 touchdowns.

The 1925 season also saw the NFL introduce a new playoff format, with the top four teams from the regular season competing in a two-round tournament to determine the league champion. The playoff system was a success, drawing large crowds and generating excitement among fans.

One of the most memorable games of the 1925 season was the Thanksgiving Day matchup between the Chicago Bears and the Detroit Panthers. The game was played in front of a record crowd of 36,000 fans at the University of Detroit Stadium, and it was a high-scoring affair that saw the Bears emerge with a 0-0 tie. Despite the lack of a winner, the game was widely regarded as a showcase for the NFL and helped solidify the league's popularity in the eyes of the public.

Off the field, the NFL continued to grapple with issues of player safety and financial stability. In 1925, the league introduced a rule requiring players to wear leather helmets, which provided more protection than the soft leather caps that had been worn previously. However, many players still chose to go without helmets, and the league struggled to enforce the new rule.

In addition, several teams faced financial difficulties during the 1925 season, with the Hammond Pros and the Milwaukee Badgers both folding mid-season due to lack of funds. The NFL responded by instituting a franchise fee for new teams, which helped to ensure the financial stability of the league going forward.

Despite these challenges, the NFL continued to grow and establish itself as a major force in American sports. The success of the 1925 season, both on and off the field, set the stage for further expansion and development in the years to come.

1926

The year 1926 was an important one for the NFL, as the league continued to grow and expand in popularity across the country. The NFL had established itself as the premier professional football organization in America, and the 1926 season saw a number of exciting developments both on and off the field.

One of the standout teams of the 1926 season was the Frankford Yellow Jackets, who finished the season with a record of 14 wins, 1 loss, and 2 ties. Led by player-coach Guy Chamberlin, the Yellow Jackets featured a dominant defense and a balanced offense, and they defeated the Chicago Bears in the NFL championship game to claim the league title.

The 1926 season also saw the NFL expand to 22 teams, with new franchises in Providence, Rhode Island, and Orange, New Jersey, among others. This expansion was a testament to the growing popularity of professional football and the increasing demand for more teams and games.

Off the field, the NFL continued to grapple with issues of player safety and financial stability. In 1926, the league introduced a new rule requiring players to wear helmets with a hard outer shell, which provided more protection than the leather helmets that had been worn previously. However, many players still chose to go without helmets, and the league struggled to enforce the new rule.

In addition, several teams faced financial difficulties during the 1926 season, with the Los Angeles Buccaneers and the Brooklyn Lions both folding mid-season due to lack of funds. The NFL responded by instituting more stringent financial requirements for new teams, in an effort to ensure the long-term stability of the league.

One of the most memorable moments of the 1926 season came in a game between the Pottsville Maroons and the Chicago Cardinals. The Maroons defeated the Cardinals on the field, but were later stripped of their win and their NFL membership for playing an unauthorized game against a team from outside the league. The controversy surrounding this decision led to a rift within the NFL and a loss of credibility among fans.

Despite this setback, the NFL continued to grow and expand, with new teams and new fans joining the fold each year. The league was still far from the lucrative business it would become in later decades, but the seeds of success had been planted, and the NFL was on its way to becoming one of the most popular and lucrative professional sports organizations in the world.

1927

The year 1927 was a landmark year for the NFL, as the league continued to grow in popularity and prestige across the country. The 1927 season saw several important developments both on and off the field, as the NFL continued its quest to establish itself as the premier professional football organization in America.

One of the standout teams of the 1927 season was the New York Giants, who finished the year with a record of 11 wins, 1 loss, and 1 tie. The Giants were led by head coach Earl Potteiger and featured a potent offense led by quarterback Hap Moran and halfback Hinkey Haines. The team won the NFL championship game against the Chicago Bears, solidifying their place as one of the dominant teams in the league.

The 1927 season also saw the NFL expand once again, with new franchises in Orange, New Jersey, and Cincinnati, Ohio, among others. This expansion was a testament to the growing popularity of professional football and the increasing demand for more teams and games.

Off the field, the NFL continued to face challenges related to player safety and financial stability. In 1927, the league introduced a new rule requiring players to wear helmets at all times during games, a rule that was finally enforced more effectively than in previous seasons. However, many players still chose to go without helmets, and the league continued to struggle with the issue of player safety.

In addition, several teams faced financial difficulties during the 1927 season, with the Dayton Triangles and the Buffalo Bisons both folding mid-season due to lack of funds. The NFL responded by instituting even stricter financial requirements for new teams, in an effort to ensure the long-term stability of the league.

One of the most memorable moments of the 1927 season came in a game between the Chicago Cardinals and the Milwaukee Badgers. The Badgers, who were one of the weaker teams in the league, managed to defeat the Cardinals in a thrilling upset that stunned the football world. The victory helped to establish the Badgers as a team to be reckoned with, and it demonstrated the unpredictable nature of the NFL and the excitement it could generate.

Despite the challenges and setbacks, the NFL continued to grow and expand in the late 1920s, establishing itself as a major force in American sports. The league was still far from the lucrative business it would become in later decades, but the foundations had been laid, and the NFL was on its way to becoming one of the most popular and profitable professional sports organizations in the world.

1928

The year 1928 was a pivotal one for the NFL, as the league continued to grow and evolve in exciting new ways. The 1928 season saw several important developments both on and off the field, as the NFL continued to establish itself as the premier professional football organization in America.

One of the standout teams of the 1928 season was the Providence Steam Roller, who finished the year with a record of 8 wins, 1 loss, and 2 ties. The Steam Roller were led by head coach Jimmy Conzelman and featured a talented roster that included quarterback Joe Bach, fullback Jim Musick, and halfback Eddie Casey. The team defeated the Frankford Yellow Jackets in the NFL championship game, cementing their place as one of the top teams in the league.

The 1928 season also saw the NFL expand once again, with new franchises in Buffalo, New York, and Detroit, Michigan, among others. This expansion was a testament to the growing popularity of professional football and the increasing demand for more teams and games.

Off the field, the NFL faced several important challenges related to player safety and financial stability. In 1928, the league introduced a new rule requiring players to wear helmets with a chin strap, providing even more protection than the hard-shell helmets that had been required in previous seasons. However, many players still chose to go without helmets, and the league continued to struggle with the issue of player safety.

In addition, several teams faced financial difficulties during the 1928 season, with the Buffalo Bisons folding mid-season for the second year in a row due to lack of funds. The NFL responded by instituting even stricter financial requirements for new teams, in an effort to ensure the long-term stability of the league.

One of the most memorable moments of the 1928 season came in a game between the Chicago Cardinals and the Chicago Bears, two bitter rivals in one of the league's most heated rivalries. In a hard-fought game that went down to the wire, the Cardinals managed to upset the heavily favored Bears in front of a raucous crowd, igniting celebrations throughout the city.

Despite the challenges and setbacks, the NFL continued to grow and expand in the late 1920s, establishing itself as a major force in American sports. The league was still far from the lucrative business it would become in later decades, but the foundations had been laid, and the NFL was on its way to becoming one of the most popular and profitable professional sports organizations in the world.

1929

The year 1929 was a significant one for the NFL, as the league continued to expand and establish itself as a major force in American sports. The 1929 season saw several important developments both on and off the field, as the NFL continued to grow in popularity and prestige.

One of the standout teams of the 1929 season was the Green Bay Packers, who finished the year with a record of 12 wins, 0 losses, and 1 tie. The Packers were led by legendary head coach Curly Lambeau and featured a talented roster that included quarterback Red Dunn, fullback Johnny McNally, and halfback Verne Lewellen. The team defeated the New York Giants in the NFL championship game, completing the first undefeated and untied season in NFL history.

The 1929 season also saw the NFL expand once again, with new franchises in Staten Island, New York, and Newark, New Jersey, among others. This expansion was a testament to the growing popularity of professional football and the increasing demand for more teams and games.

Off the field, the NFL faced several important challenges related to player safety and financial stability. In 1929, the league introduced a new rule requiring all players to wear helmets during games, with a heavy emphasis on safety and protection. This was a significant step forward for the league, which had struggled in previous years with players who refused to wear helmets or who wore inadequate protection.

In addition, several teams faced financial difficulties during the 1929 season, with the Orange Tornadoes and the Staten Island Stapletons both folding mid-season due to lack of funds. The NFL responded by instituting even stricter financial requirements for new teams, in an effort to ensure the long-term stability of the league.

One of the most memorable moments of the 1929 season came in a game between the Chicago Bears and the Portsmouth Spartans, two of the top teams in the league. In a hard-fought game that went down to the wire, the Bears managed to defeat the Spartans in a controversial finish that saw the Bears score a touchdown on the last play of the game. The outcome of the game was a major point of contention and sparked widespread debate and discussion throughout the league and the sports world.

Despite the challenges and setbacks, the NFL continued to grow and expand in the late 1920s, establishing itself as a major force in American sports. The league was still far from the lucrative business it would become in later decades, but the foundations had been laid, and the NFL was on its way to becoming one of the most popular and profitable professional sports organizations in the world.

THE 1930'S

1930

The year 1930 marked a turning point in the history of the NFL, as the league faced several significant challenges both on and off the field. The 1930 season saw the NFL grapple with issues related to player safety, financial stability, and competitive balance, as the league continued to evolve and expand.

One of the standout teams of the 1930 season was the Green Bay Packers, who continued their dominance from the previous year with a record of 10 wins, 3 losses, and 1 tie. The Packers were led once again by head coach Curly Lambeau and featured a talented roster that included quarterback Red Dunn, fullback Johnny McNally, and halfback Verne Lewellen. The team defeated the New York Giants in the NFL championship game for the second year in a row, cementing their place as one of the greatest teams in NFL history.

The 1930 season also saw the NFL expand once again, with new franchises in Brooklyn, New York, and Portsmouth, Ohio, among others. This expansion was a testament to the growing popularity of professional football and the increasing demand for more teams and games.

Off the field, the NFL faced several important challenges related to player safety and financial stability. In 1930, the league instituted a new rule prohibiting players from wearing helmets with dangerous protrusions or spikes, further emphasizing the importance of safety and protection for players. In addition, several teams faced financial difficulties during the 1930 season, with the Cleveland Indians and the Newark Tornadoes both folding mid-season due to lack of funds. The NFL responded by implementing even stricter financial requirements for new teams, in an effort to ensure the long-term stability of the league.

One of the biggest controversies of the 1930 season came in a game between the Green Bay Packers and the New York Giants, two of the top teams in the league. In a closely contested game, the Giants were called for a disputed penalty that many believed cost them the game. The outcome of the game sparked widespread debate and discussion throughout the league and the sports world, highlighting the importance of fair and impartial officiating in professional football.

Another important development in the 1930 season was the introduction of the unofficial NFL Championship Trophy, which was awarded to the team with the best record at the end of the season. This trophy would eventually become the Vince Lombardi Trophy, the official championship trophy of the NFL.

Overall, the 1930 season was a challenging one for the NFL, as the league faced significant obstacles related to safety, finances, and competitiveness. However, the league continued to grow and evolve, with more teams, more games, and more fans than ever before. The NFL was on its way to becoming the premier professional football organization in America, setting the stage for the decades of success and growth that would follow.

1931

The year 1931 was a significant one for the NFL, as the league continued to evolve and adapt to the changing landscape of professional football in America. The 1931 season saw the introduction of several important changes and innovations, as the NFL sought to enhance the fan experience, improve player safety, and ensure the long-term stability of the league.

One of the biggest changes in the 1931 season was the introduction of night games, which allowed fans to attend games after work and provided a new level of excitement and spectacle to professional football. The first night game was played on November 21, 1931, between the Philadelphia Eagles and the Chicago Cardinals, with the Eagles winning 7-6. The success of the first night game paved the way for more night games in future seasons, and the NFL would eventually become known for its prime-time television broadcasts.

Another important development in the 1931 season was the implementation of new rules related to player safety. The NFL continued to emphasize the importance of protecting players from dangerous hits and injuries, and instituted new penalties for actions that were deemed to be unnecessarily violent or dangerous. These rules helped to ensure that players could compete at the highest level without putting themselves at undue risk, and helped to set the stage for the modern emphasis on player safety that continues to this day.

On the field, the 1931 season was marked by a highly competitive race for the NFL championship. The Green Bay Packers, who had won the championship in 1929 and 1930, were once again one of the top teams in the league, with a record of 12 wins and 2 losses. However, the Packers faced stiff competition from the Portsmouth Spartans, who finished the season with a record of 11 wins, 3 losses, and 1 tie. The two teams met in the NFL championship game, which was played at the University of Chicago's Stagg Field on December 13, 1931. The game was a tightly contested affair, with the Packers ultimately prevailing by a score of 12-0.

Off the field, the NFL continued to face financial challenges related to the Great Depression, which had a significant impact on the economy and on professional sports. Several teams struggled financially, and some were forced to fold or merge with other teams in order to stay afloat. However, the league continued to expand and evolve, with new teams in Boston, Staten Island, and Brooklyn, among others.

Overall, the 1931 season was a pivotal one for the NFL, as the league continued to grow and adapt to the changing needs and expectations of professional football in America. The introduction of night games, the emphasis on player safety, and the highly competitive race for the NFL championship all helped to cement the league's place as a major force in American sports, and set the stage for the decades of success and growth that would follow.

1932

The year 1932 marked the beginning of a new era in American football, with the league expanding to ten teams and introducing several new rules to the game. This section explores the key events and developments that shaped the NFL in 1932.

Expansion of the NFL

In 1932, the NFL expanded to ten teams with the addition of the Pittsburgh Pirates (now the Pittsburgh Steelers) and the Philadelphia Eagles. The Pirates were owned by Art Rooney, who had previously owned a semi-professional team in Pittsburgh. The Eagles, on the other hand, were owned by a group of investors led by Bert Bell and Lud Wray.

The addition of these two teams marked a significant shift in the NFL's power balance, as it allowed teams in the Eastern United States to compete with those in the Midwest and West. The expansion also brought the NFL one step closer to becoming a true national league, with teams located across the country.

New Rules

1932 was a year of significant rule changes in the NFL. The most notable change was the introduction of the forward pass, which had previously been heavily restricted. The new rules allowed quarterbacks to throw the ball from anywhere behind the line of scrimmage, and receivers were allowed to catch the ball as long as they were onside.

Other rule changes included the adoption of the 15-yard penalty for roughing the passer and the requirement that a team must gain at least ten yards in three plays to earn a first down. These changes helped to make the game more exciting and opened up new opportunities for offensive play.

Championship Game

The 1932 NFL Championship Game was played between the Chicago Bears and the Portsmouth Spartans (now the Detroit Lions) on December 18, 1932. The game was notable for several reasons, including the fact that it was the first NFL Championship Game to be decided in overtime.

The game ended in a 7-7 tie after regulation time, and a decision was made to play an additional 15-minute period.

The Bears scored a field goal in the extra period to win the game 10-7 and claim their second consecutive NFL championship.

The year 1932 was a pivotal year in the history of the NFL. The expansion of the league to ten teams and the introduction of new rules helped to establish the NFL as a truly national sport. The 1932 NFL Championship Game was also a significant moment in the league's history, paving the way for future playoff games and overtime rules.

1933

The year 1933 was a transformative year for the NFL. Following the successful expansion to ten teams in 1932, the league continued to evolve and grow in popularity. This chapter explores the key events and developments that shaped the NFL in 1933.

Divisional Play

In 1933, the NFL introduced divisional play for the first time. The league was split into two divisions - the Eastern Division and the Western Division - with each division consisting of five teams. The winners of each division would then play each other in the NFL Championship Game.

This new structure helped to create more intense rivalries within the league and provided fans with a greater sense of excitement and anticipation. It also allowed teams from different parts of the country to play against each other more frequently.

New Teams

The 1933 NFL season saw the addition of three new teams to the league - the Cincinnati Reds, the Philadelphia Eagles, and the Pittsburgh Pirates (now the Pittsburgh Steelers). The inclusion of these teams brought the number of teams in the league to 11, further expanding the league's reach and fan base.

The Cincinnati Reds were owned by local businessman George E. Thayer and played their home games at Crosley Field. The Eagles and Pirates both returned to the league after a brief hiatus, with the Eagles being purchased by Bert Bell and Lud Wray and the Pirates being owned by Art Rooney.

NFL Championship Game

The 1933 NFL Championship Game was played on December 17, 1933, between the Chicago Bears and the New York Giants. The game was played at Wrigley Field in Chicago and was attended by over 26,000 fans.

The Bears dominated the game, winning by a score of 23-21. The victory marked the team's third NFL championship in four years, cementing their status as one of the dominant teams of the early NFL era.

The year 1933 was another significant year in the history of the NFL. The introduction of divisional play helped to create more excitement and rivalries within the league, while the addition of new teams further expanded the NFL's reach and fan base. The 1933 NFL Championship Game also marked a key moment in the league's history, with the Chicago Bears establishing themselves as one of the dominant teams of the era.

1934

The year 1934 marked another year of growth and evolution for the NFL. Following the success of the previous two seasons, the league continued to expand and attract new fans.

New Teams

The NFL continued to expand in 1934 with the addition of two new teams - the Cincinnati Reds and the St. Louis Gunners. The Cincinnati Reds had joined the league in 1933 but struggled to compete and finished with a record of just 3-6-1. The St. Louis Gunners were owned by Bernie Bierman, a former football player and coach, and played their home games at Sportsman's Park.

The inclusion of these new teams helped to further expand the NFL's reach and popularity, particularly in the Midwest and Southeast regions of the United States.

Racial Integration

1934 was also a significant year for racial integration in the NFL. Kenny Washington, a talented running back from UCLA, was signed by the Los Angeles Bulldogs of the Pacific Coast Professional Football League (PCPFL). This made him the first African-American player to sign a professional football contract since the 1920s.

Despite his success in the PCPFL, Washington was initially unable to secure a contract with an NFL team due to the league's unwritten ban on black players. However, his signing helped to break down barriers and pave the way for other black players to enter the NFL in the years to come.

NFL Championship Game

The 1934 NFL Championship Game was played on December 9, 1934, between the New York Giants and the Chicago Bears. The game was played at the Polo Grounds in New York and was attended by over 35,000 fans.

The Giants dominated the game, winning by a score of 30-13. The victory marked the team's first NFL championship and established them as one of the dominant teams of the era.

The year 1934 was another important year in the history of the NFL. The addition of new teams helped to expand the league's reach and popularity, while the signing of Kenny Washington helped to break down racial barriers and pave the way for future integration. The 1934 NFL Championship Game also marked a key moment in the league's history, with the New York Giants establishing themselves as a dominant force in the NFL.

1935

The year 1935 was a year of significant changes for the NFL. With the league continuing to expand and evolve, new rules and regulations were introduced, and the game continued to gain popularity across the United States.

New Rules and Regulations

The NFL introduced several new rules and regulations in 1935 to help improve player safety and increase the flow of the game. One of the most significant changes was the adoption of the 15-yard penalty for pass interference, which helped to make the passing game a more viable option for teams.

Other rule changes included the introduction of a maximum roster size of 22 players, the removal of the drop kick from kickoffs, and the elimination of the penalty for a forward pass that went incomplete beyond the line of scrimmage.

Expansion of the NFL Draft

The NFL Draft, which had been introduced in 1936, was expanded in 1935 to include all NFL teams. Previously, the draft had only been open to teams that finished at the bottom of the league standings, with the aim of promoting competitive balance.

The expansion of the draft allowed all teams to participate in the selection process, with the draft order determined by a random selection. This helped to ensure that all teams had an equal opportunity to improve their rosters and compete for a championship.

NFL Championship Game

The 1935 NFL Championship Game was played on December 15, 1935, between the Detroit Lions and the New York Giants. The game was played at the University of Detroit Stadium and was attended by over 15,000 fans.

The Lions dominated the game, winning by a score of 26-7. The victory marked the team's first NFL championship and established them as a rising force in the league.

The year 1935 was an important year in the history of the NFL. The introduction of new rules and regulations helped to improve player safety and increase the flow of the game, while the expansion of the NFL Draft ensured that all teams had an equal opportunity to improve their rosters.

The 1935 NFL Championship Game also marked a key moment in the league's history, with the Detroit Lions establishing themselves as a rising force in the NFL.

1936

The year 1936 marked a significant turning point for the NFL. With the league continuing to expand and evolve, 1936 saw the introduction of the NFL Draft, which would help to shape the league for decades to come.

Introduction of the NFL Draft

The NFL Draft was introduced in 1936 as a way to promote competitive balance in the league. The draft was designed to ensure that the worst teams from the previous season would have the first opportunity to select new players, thus providing them with a chance to improve their rosters.

The first NFL Draft was held on February 8, 1936, with the Philadelphia Eagles selecting Jay Berwanger, a running back from the University of Chicago, as the first overall pick. The draft was conducted over nine rounds, with each team given one pick per round.

The introduction of the NFL Draft was a significant moment in the league's history, and it would go on to become one of the defining features of the NFL.

New Teams

The NFL continued to expand in 1936 with the addition of two new teams - the Pittsburgh Pirates and the Boston Redskins. The Pittsburgh Pirates had been previously known as the Pittsburgh Steelers, but changed their name to avoid confusion with the city's baseball team.

The Boston Redskins, meanwhile, had relocated from Boston to Washington, D.C., and would go on to become the Washington Redskins. The inclusion of these new teams helped to further expand the NFL's reach and popularity.

NFL Championship Game

The 1936 NFL Championship Game was played on December 13, 1936, between the Green Bay Packers and the Boston Redskins. The game was played at the Polo Grounds in New York and was attended by over 29,000 fans.

The Packers dominated the game, winning by a score of 21-6. The victory marked the team's fourth NFL championship and established them as one of the dominant teams of the era.

The year 1936 was an important year in the history of the NFL. The introduction of the NFL Draft helped to promote competitive balance in the league and would go on to become one of the defining features of the NFL. The addition of new teams further expanded the league's reach and popularity, while the 1936 NFL Championship Game saw the Green Bay Packers establish themselves as one of the dominant teams of the era.

1937

The year 1937 was a tumultuous one for the NFL. With a number of key developments taking place, including the introduction of a new team and the departure of one of the league's most iconic coaches, the year marked a turning point in the league's history.

Washington Redskins Win First Championship

The 1937 NFL Championship Game saw the Washington Redskins win their first-ever title, defeating the Chicago

Bears by a score of 28-21. The game was played at Wrigley Field in Chicago and was attended by over 15,000 fans.

The victory was a significant moment in the history of the Redskins, who had only joined the league in 1932. Led by quarterback Sammy Baugh, the Redskins dominated the game, with Baugh throwing three touchdown passes to secure the win.

Despite their victory, the Redskins would not return to the championship game for another 25 years, but the win marked the start of a successful period for the team.

Bronko Nagurski Retires

One of the biggest stories of the year was the retirement of Bronko Nagurski, one of the most iconic players in NFL history. Nagurski had played for the Chicago Bears since 1930 and had become famous for his physical and aggressive style of play.

Despite being only 29 years old, Nagurski announced his retirement from football in 1937, citing a desire to focus on his wrestling career. Nagurski would go on to have a successful wrestling career, but his retirement was a significant loss for the NFL and the Chicago Bears.

New Team: Cleveland Rams

The NFL continued to expand in 1937 with the addition of a new team, the Cleveland Rams. The team was owned by Homer Marshman and would go on to become one of the most successful teams of the era.

The inclusion of the Cleveland Rams helped to further expand the NFL's reach and popularity, and the team quickly established itself as a force to be reckoned with in the league.

The year 1937 was a significant one for the NFL, marked by a number of key events and developments. The Washington Redskins' victory in the NFL Championship Game marked the start of a successful period for the team, while the retirement of Bronko Nagurski marked the end of an era for the Chicago Bears.

The addition of the Cleveland Rams helped to further expand the league's reach and popularity, and the team quickly established itself as a contender in the NFL. Despite the challenges and changes of the year, the NFL continued to grow and evolve, setting the stage for the future of the league.

1938

The year 1938 marked a significant moment in the history of the NFL. With the league expanding and evolving, new stars emerged and old legends continued to make their mark.

New Team

Pittsburgh Pirates Become Pittsburgh Steelers In 1938, the Pittsburgh Pirates changed their name to the Pittsburgh Steelers, adopting the name of the city's thriving steel industry. The change came after the team was bought by Art Rooney, who had been instrumental in the development of football in Pittsburgh.

The name change was a significant moment for the team, as it marked a new era for the franchise. Under Rooney's leadership, the Steelers would go on to become one of the most successful teams in the NFL, winning multiple championships over the years.

Chicago Bears Win Fourth Championship

The Chicago Bears continued their dominance in the NFL in 1938, winning their fourth championship in just nine years. Led by coach George Halas and a talented roster of players, the Bears were the team to beat in the league.

In the championship game, the Bears defeated the New York Giants by a score of 23-21, in what was a tightly contested match. The victory cemented the Bears' place as one of the greatest teams in NFL history.

Sammy Baugh Emerges as a Star

Sammy Baugh, the quarterback for the Washington Redskins, emerged as one of the biggest stars of the 1938 NFL season. Baugh had made a name for himself the previous year, leading the Redskins to their first championship, but in 1938, he took his game to the next level.

Baugh led the league in passing yards and touchdowns, establishing himself as one of the most talented quarterbacks in the game. His success helped to further popularize the forward pass and revolutionized the way that the game was played.

The year 1938 was a significant one for the NFL, marked by a number of key events and developments. The name change of the Pittsburgh Pirates to the Pittsburgh Steelers marked the start of a new era for the franchise, while the Chicago Bears' continued dominance in the league cemented their place as one of the greatest teams in NFL history.

Sammy Baugh's emergence as a star helped to further popularize the forward pass and revolutionized the way that the game was played. With the league expanding and evolving, the stage was set for the NFL to continue to grow and thrive in the years to come.

1939

The year 1939 marked the end of a decade that had seen the NFL evolve and grow in popularity. As the league expanded and new stars emerged, the game of football began to captivate audiences across the country.

Expansion: Philadelphia Eagles Join the League

In 1939, the NFL expanded again with the addition of a new team, the Philadelphia Eagles. The team was founded by Bert Bell, who had previously owned the Pittsburgh Steelers. The Eagles were the first NFL team to be based in Philadelphia since the Frankford Yellow Jackets folded in 1931.

The addition of the Eagles brought the total number of teams in the league to nine, and the move was seen as a positive step forward for the NFL's growth and expansion.

Chicago Bears Win Fifth Championship

The Chicago Bears continued their dominance in the NFL in 1939, winning their fifth championship in just ten years. Led by legendary coach George Halas and a talented roster of players, the Bears were once again the team to beat in the league.

In the championship game, the Bears defeated the Washington Redskins by a score of 73-0, in what remains the most lopsided victory in NFL history. The win cemented the Bears' place as one of the greatest teams in NFL history.

Joe Stydahar Emerges as a Star

Joe Stydahar, an offensive tackle for the Chicago Bears, emerged as one of the biggest stars of the 1939 NFL season. Stydahar had been drafted by the Bears the previous year and had quickly established himself as a talented player.

In 1939, Stydahar helped to anchor the Bears' dominant offensive line, which was one of the key factors in the team's success. His performance earned him All-Pro honors and helped to establish him as one of the best offensive linemen in the league.

The year 1939 was a significant one for the NFL, marked by the addition of a new team, the Philadelphia Eagles, and the continued dominance of the Chicago Bears. The Bears' fifth championship victory cemented their place as one of the greatest teams in NFL history, while Joe Stydahar's emergence as a star helped to establish him as one of the best offensive linemen in the league.

With the NFL continuing to expand and evolve, the stage was set for the league to enter a new decade of growth and popularity. The game of football had firmly established itself as one of America's favorite pastimes, and the NFL was poised to become a cultural institution in the years to come.

THE 1940'S

1940

The year 1940 was an important one for the NFL. The league continued to grow in popularity, with more fans tuning in to watch their favorite teams compete.

Expansion: Pittsburgh Steelers Join the League

In 1940, the NFL expanded once again with the addition of the Pittsburgh Steelers. The team had previously played in the Eastern Division of the third American Football League (AFL) and was owned by Art Rooney.

The Steelers brought the total number of teams in the NFL to ten, and the move was seen as a positive step forward for the league's growth and expansion.

Chicago Bears Win Sixth Championship

The Chicago Bears continued their dominance in the NFL in 1940, winning their sixth championship in just eleven years. The team was led once again by legendary coach George Halas, and featured a talented roster of players.

In the championship game, the Bears defeated the Washington Redskins by a score of 73-0, in a rematch of the previous year's title game. The win cemented the Bears' place as one of the greatest teams in NFL history.

Sid Luckman Emerges as a Star

Sid Luckman, a quarterback for the Chicago Bears, emerged as one of the biggest stars of the 1940 NFL season. Luckman had been drafted by the Bears in 1939, and had initially struggled to adapt to the pro game.

In 1940, Luckman began to find his stride, leading the Bears to an 8-3 record and a championship victory. His performance in the championship game, where he threw for five touchdowns, helped to establish him as one of the best quarterbacks in the league.

The Birth of the Pro Bowl

In 1940, the NFL held its first-ever Pro Bowl game, featuring the league's top players from each conference. The game was played in Los Angeles, California, and featured a sellout crowd of 21,000 fans.

The inaugural Pro Bowl was a success, and the game has since become an annual tradition in the NFL. It has also been used as a showcase for some of the league's top talent, and is often seen as a sign of a player's status as one of the best in the game.

The year 1940 was an important one for the NFL, marked by the addition of a new team, the Pittsburgh Steelers, and the continued dominance of the Chicago Bears. The Bears' sixth championship victory cemented their place as one of the greatest teams in NFL history, while Sid Luckman's emergence as a star helped to establish him as one of the best quarterbacks in the league.

The birth of the Pro Bowl also marked a significant milestone in the history of the NFL, as the league continued to expand and evolve. With more fans tuning in to watch their favorite teams, the NFL was poised to enter a new decade of growth and popularity.

1941: A Season of Change and Challenges

The year 1941 was a significant year in the history of the NFL. It was a year of change, challenges, and transformation as the country was on the verge of entering World War II. The NFL had to deal with many challenges during the season, including player shortages, game cancellations, and financial difficulties. Nevertheless, the league managed to overcome these challenges and deliver an exciting season of football.

Player Shortages

The NFL faced player shortages in 1941 as many players were called to serve in the military. This led to a decline in the quality of play on the field as teams struggled to find replacements for their star players. Additionally, some teams had to merge to form a single team due to a lack of players. For example, the Philadelphia Eagles and Pittsburgh Steelers merged to form the "Steagles" for the 1943 season.

Game Cancellations

The outbreak of World War II also affected the NFL's schedule as several games had to be canceled due to travel restrictions and safety concerns. The league also had to deal with the challenge of scheduling games around military service obligations. For example, the Detroit Lions played their first game of the season on October 19, 1941, because the team's star player, Dutch Clark, had military obligations.

Financial Difficulties

The war also affected the NFL's financial stability as attendance at games declined due to the economic constraints of the time. The league's revenue also declined as teams had to spend more money on travel and accommodation expenses. Nevertheless, the NFL managed to stay afloat by implementing cost-cutting measures and introducing new revenue streams, such as radio broadcasts of games.

The 1941 NFL Season

Despite the challenges faced by the league, the 1941 NFL season was an exciting one. The Chicago Bears dominated the regular season, finishing with a 10-1 record. The team's star running back, Bill Osmanski, led the league in rushing with 699 yards. The New York Giants also had a strong season, finishing with an 8-3 record. The Giants' defense was one of the best in the league, allowing only 107 points in 11 games.

The NFL Championship Game was played on December 21, 1941, just two weeks after the attack on Pearl Harbor. The game was between the Chicago Bears and the New York Giants and was played at Wrigley Field in Chicago. Despite the challenges of the time, over 13,000 fans attended the game. The Bears won the game 37-9, with quarterback Sid Luckman throwing three touchdown passes.

The year 1941 was a challenging one for the NFL as the country was on the brink of war. The league had to deal with player shortages, game cancellations, and financial difficulties. Nevertheless, the NFL managed to deliver an exciting season of football that provided a welcome distraction for fans during a difficult time. The 1941 season was a testament to the resilience of the NFL and its ability to overcome challenges and adversity.

1942

The year 1942 marked the second season of the NFL during World War II. The league had to adapt to a new reality in which many players and fans were serving in the military, and the country was focused on the war effort. The 1942 NFL season was a season of adaptation and sacrifice, as the league continued to provide entertainment to the American people while also contributing to the war effort.

Player Shortages

The player shortages that plagued the NFL in 1941 continued into the 1942 season. Many of the league's star players were called to serve in the military, and teams had to rely on inexperienced or untested players. As a result, the quality of play suffered, and teams struggled to compete. However, the league continued to hold games, and fans turned out to support their teams.

Game Scheduling

The war also affected the NFL's scheduling of games in 1942. The league had to work around military obligations and travel restrictions, which led to some games being played on weekdays rather than weekends. In addition, the league had to cancel several games due to travel restrictions and other logistical issues. Despite these challenges, the NFL managed to complete a full season of games.

Financial Challenges

The war also affected the NFL's financial stability in 1942. Attendance at games declined, and the league's revenue decreased. However, the NFL managed to stay afloat by introducing new revenue streams, such as radio broadcasts of games. In addition, the league worked to reduce costs by cutting back on travel expenses and other expenses.

The 1942 NFL Season

The 1942 NFL season was a season of adaptation and sacrifice, as the league and its teams worked to contribute to the war effort while also providing entertainment to the American people. Despite the challenges, the season was marked by several notable moments and achievements.

The Washington Redskins, led by quarterback Sammy Baugh, won their second NFL championship, defeating the Chicago Bears 14-6 in the championship game. Baugh, who was also a punter and defensive back, was one of the few star players who continued to play in the NFL during the war. He was a true hero of the game, demonstrating courage and resilience both on and off the field.

Another notable moment of the 1942 season was the debut of African American players in the NFL. The Cleveland Rams signed two black players, Kenny Washington and Woody Strode, in the spring of 1946, breaking the league's color barrier. Although Washington and Strode faced racism and discrimination, their presence in the league paved the way for future generations of African American players.

The 1942 NFL season was a season of adaptation and sacrifice, as the league and its teams worked to contribute to the war effort while also providing entertainment to the American people. The league continued to face challenges, including player shortages, game scheduling issues, and financial difficulties. However, the NFL managed to overcome these challenges and deliver a season of football that provided a much-needed distraction from the war. The 1942 season demonstrated the resilience of the NFL and its ability to adapt to changing circumstances.

1943

The year 1943 was a tumultuous time for the United States, as the country was fully committed to World War II. The NFL was not immune to the effects of the war, as many players, coaches, and team personnel were either drafted or enlisted in the military. This resulted in a number of changes to the NFL's structure, rules, and personnel during the 1943 season.

The War Effort and the NFL

The war effort had a profound impact on the NFL in 1943. With so many players and coaches serving in the military, many teams were left with depleted rosters. To address this issue, the NFL allowed teams to merge for the 1943 season. This resulted in the formation of the "Steagles," a team made up of players from the Pittsburgh Steelers and Philadelphia Eagles, and the "Card-Pitt" team, made up of players from the Chicago Cardinals and Pittsburgh Steelers. Both teams struggled on the field, with the Steagles finishing with a 5-4-1 record and Card-Pitt finishing with a 0-10 record.

In addition to the mergers, the NFL also implemented a number of other changes to help maintain competitive balance during the war years. The league instituted a "player draft pool," which allowed teams to select players from a common pool of available talent. This ensured that the best players were distributed evenly across the league, rather than being concentrated on a few teams. The NFL also relaxed its eligibility rules, allowing players who were not currently enrolled in college to play in the league.

The Impact on Individual Teams

The war had a profound impact on individual NFL teams as well. The Chicago Bears, for example, lost several key players to the military, including star quarterback Sid

Luckman. Despite this, the team managed to finish the season with an 8-1-1 record and win the NFL championship. The Washington Redskins, on the other hand, lost so many players to the military that they were forced to suspend operations for the 1943 season.

The war also impacted the way that individual teams played on the field. With many of the league's best players serving in the military, teams had to rely on younger, less experienced players. This often resulted in a more conservative style of play, with teams focusing on running the ball and playing solid defense.

The Legacy of 1943

The 1943 NFL season was a unique and challenging time for the league. The war effort forced teams to adapt and change, and many players and coaches sacrificed their careers to serve their country. Despite the difficulties, the NFL managed to survive and even thrive during the war years, laying the groundwork for the league's future success.

Looking back, the 1943 season serves as a reminder of the sacrifices made by so many during World War II. It also shows the resilience of the NFL and its ability to adapt to changing circumstances. While the 1943 season may not be remembered for its great performances or individual accomplishments, it remains an important chapter in the league's history and a testament to the courage and dedication of those who played a part in it.

1944

The year 1944 marked the second consecutive year in which the NFL was heavily impacted by World War II. With many players, coaches, and team personnel still serving in the military, the league continued to face significant challenges. Despite these difficulties, the 1944 season was a pivotal one in the history of the NFL, with several key developments that would shape the league for years to come.

The War Effort and the NFL

As in 1943, the war effort had a significant impact on the NFL in 1944. Many players and coaches were still serving in the military, and several teams were forced to merge in order to field competitive rosters. The Cleveland Rams and the Pittsburgh Steelers, for example, merged to form the "Cardinals-Steelers" team, which played its home games in Pittsburgh. The team finished with a 0-10 record, illustrating the difficulties of fielding a competitive team in the midst of the war.

Despite these challenges, the NFL continued to make efforts to maintain competitive balance. The league's "player draft pool" remained in place, and the eligibility rules for players were still relaxed. However, the league also implemented a new rule that allowed teams to use an "emergency player" if they had fewer than 25 players available. This helped teams to avoid forfeiting games due to a lack of available players.

The Impact on Individual Teams

The war continued to impact individual NFL teams in 1944. The Green Bay Packers, for example, lost several key players to the military, including star quarterback Cecil Isbell. The team struggled to a 2-8 record, its worst finish in over a decade. The Chicago Bears, on the other hand, managed to maintain their dominance despite losing several players to the war effort. Led by coach George Halas and quarterback Sid Luckman, the team finished with a 6-3-1 record and won their second consecutive NFL championship.

The Legacy of 1944

The 1944 NFL season was a difficult and challenging time for the league. The war effort continued to take a toll on teams and players, and many sacrificed their careers to serve their country. However, the season was also a pivotal one in the history of the NFL. The league's efforts to maintain competitive balance and adapt to changing circumstances helped it to survive and even thrive during the war years.

Looking back, the 1944 season serves as a reminder of the sacrifices made by so many during World War II. It also highlights the resilience of the NFL and its ability to overcome adversity. While the 1944 season may not be remembered for its great performances or individual accomplishments, it remains an important chapter in the league's history and a testament to the courage and dedication of those who played a part in it.

1945

The year 1945 marked an interesting time in the history of the NFL. With World War II still raging, the league faced significant challenges in terms of player availability and fan attendance. However, the NFL managed to weather these challenges and emerge stronger than ever before.

The War Years

During the war years, the NFL faced a shortage of players as many of its star athletes were called up to serve in the military. This forced the league to rely on older and inexperienced players to fill out its rosters. In addition, many games were played on Sunday mornings to accommodate wartime work schedules. Despite these challenges, the league managed to continue playing throughout the war years, albeit with reduced rosters and attendance.

The Cleveland Rams

One of the most interesting stories of the 1945 NFL season was the relocation of the Cleveland Rams to Los Angeles. The Rams had struggled financially in Cleveland, and owner Dan Reeves decided to move the team to California. The move was not without controversy, as several NFL owners opposed the relocation. However, Reeves was able to convince a majority of the league's owners to approve the move, and the Rams became the first NFL team on the West Coast.

The Championship Game

The 1945 NFL Championship Game featured the Cleveland Rams against the Washington Redskins. The game was played on December 16, 1945, in Cleveland, Ohio. The Rams won the game 15-14, thanks in large part to a 30-yard field goal by Jim Gillette with just over two minutes remaining in the game.

The championship game was a closely contested affair, with both teams trading blows throughout the game. The Redskins took an early lead in the first quarter when quarterback Sammy Baugh connected with receiver Joe Aguirre on a 35-yard touchdown pass. The Rams responded with a touchdown of their own in the second quarter, as quarterback Bob Waterfield hit receiver Jim Benton on a 19-yard scoring strike.

The Redskins regained the lead in the third quarter when Baugh found Aguirre again, this time on a 55-yard touchdown pass. The Rams answered back with a touchdown of their own, as Waterfield found halfback Jim Gillette on a 44-yard touchdown pass. With the score tied at 14-14 late in the fourth quarter, Gillette kicked the game-winning field goal to give the Rams their first NFL championship.

Despite the challenges posed by World War II, the 1945 NFL season was a successful one. The league managed to continue playing despite player shortages and reduced attendance, and the relocation of the Cleveland Rams to Los Angeles paved the way for future expansion to the West Coast. The championship game was a thrilling affair that showcased the best of what the NFL had to offer, and it set the stage for many great seasons to come.

1946

The year 1946 marked a turning point for the NFL. With World War II over, the league was able to fully focus on rebuilding and expanding. This led to several significant changes and developments that set the stage for the modern NFL.

Expansion

In 1946, the NFL expanded to 10 teams with the addition of the All-America Football Conference (AAFC) teams: the Cleveland Browns, San Francisco 49ers, and Baltimore Colts. The AAFC was seen as a rival league to the NFL, but the two leagues eventually merged in 1950.

The Cleveland Browns were arguably the most successful team in the AAFC, winning all four league championships before joining the NFL. Led by head coach Paul Brown and quarterback Otto Graham, the Browns would go on to win three NFL championships in their first six seasons in the league.

Integration

Another significant development in 1946 was the integration of the NFL. The Los Angeles Rams signed Kenny Washington and Woody Strode, making them the first African American players to play in the NFL since 1933. The Cleveland Browns also signed Marion Motley and Bill Willis, making them the first African American players to play for an NFL team in the modern era.

Integration was not without its challenges, however. Many NFL players and fans were resistant to the idea of playing alongside or against African American players. Nevertheless, the integration of the NFL paved the way for greater diversity and inclusion in professional sports.

The Championship Game

The 1946 NFL Championship Game featured the Chicago Bears against the New York Giants. The game was played on December 15, 1946, at the Polo Grounds in New York City. The Bears won the game 24-14, thanks in large part to a dominant performance by quarterback Sid Luckman.

Luckman threw for 286 yards and three touchdowns, leading the Bears to their second NFL championship in three years. The Giants, led by quarterback Frank Filchock and running back Steve Owen, put up a valiant effort but ultimately fell short against the Bears' high-powered offense.

The year 1946 was a pivotal one for the National Football League. The expansion of the league and the integration of

African American players were significant developments that paved the way for future growth and progress. The championship game was a showcase of the best the NFL had to offer, with Sid Luckman leading the Bears to a dominant victory over the Giants. Overall, 1946 set the stage for a new era of growth and success in the NFL.

1947

The year 1947 was another important year in the history of the NFL. It was a year of continued growth and progress, both on and off the field.

The New York Yankees

One of the most interesting stories of the 1947 NFL season was the creation of the New York Yankees football team. The Yankees were owned by Dan Topping and Del Webb, who also owned the New York Yankees baseball team. The football Yankees played their home games at Yankee Stadium, sharing the stadium with the baseball Yankees.

The Yankees were not a successful team, finishing the season with a record of 2-8-1. However, they were an important addition to the league, as they helped to establish football as a major sport in New York City.

Jackie Robinson

In addition to the New York Yankees, 1947 was also the year that Jackie Robinson broke the color barrier in Major League Baseball. This was a significant event for professional sports, as it paved the way for greater racial integration and equality.

Robinson's success in baseball also had an impact on the NFL. Many NFL owners and coaches saw the success of

African American players in baseball and began to rethink their own policies regarding integration. This helped to accelerate the integration of the NFL, as more teams began to sign African American players.

The Championship Game

The 1947 NFL Championship Game featured the Chicago Cardinals against the Philadelphia Eagles. The game was played on December 28, 1947, at Comiskey Park in Chicago. The Cardinals won the game 28-21, thanks in large part to a dominant performance by quarterback Paul Christman.

Christman threw for 258 yards and two touchdowns, leading the Cardinals to their second NFL championship in team history. The Eagles, led by quarterback Tommy Thompson and running back Steve Van Buren, put up a strong fight but ultimately fell short against the Cardinals' high-powered offense.

The year 1947 was another important year in the history of the NFL. The creation of the New York Yankees helped to establish football as a major sport in New York City, while the success of Jackie Robinson in baseball paved the way for greater racial integration in professional sports. The championship game was a thrilling affair that showcased the best of what the NFL had to offer, with Paul Christman leading the Cardinals to a dominant victory over the Eagles. Overall, 1947 was a year of continued growth and progress for the NFL.

1948

The year 1948 was a continuation of the growth and progress that the NFL had experienced in the years following World War II. It was a year of exciting football, fierce competition, and important developments both on and off the field.

The AAFC Merger

One of the most significant events of 1948 was the merger of the NFL with the All-America Football Conference (AAFC). The AAFC had been established in 1946 as a rival league to the NFL, but it struggled to gain a foothold in the market. By 1948, it had become clear that the AAFC could not compete with the NFL, and negotiations began for a merger.

The merger was finalized in June of 1949, with the NFL absorbing three AAFC teams: the Cleveland Browns, the San Francisco 49ers, and the Baltimore Colts. The Browns, led by quarterback Otto Graham and head coach Paul Brown, were the most successful team in the AAFC, winning all four league championships before joining the NFL.

The Championship Game

The 1948 NFL Championship Game featured the Philadelphia Eagles against the Chicago Cardinals. The game was played on December 19, 1948, at Shibe Park in Philadelphia. The Eagles won the game 7-0, thanks in large part to a strong defensive performance and a touchdown pass from quarterback Tommy Thompson to Pete Pihos.

The Cardinals, led by quarterback Paul Christman and running back Charley Trippi, put up a strong fight but were unable to overcome the Eagles' defense. The game was a hard-fought battle that showcased the best of what the NFL had to offer.

Integration

In 1948, the NFL continued its progress towards greater racial integration. The Los Angeles Rams signed Kenny Washington and Woody Strode in 1946, breaking the color barrier in the NFL. In 1948, the Rams signed an African American player named Dan Towler, who would go on to become one of the team's top running backs.

Towler's success helped to pave the way for other African American players to be signed by NFL teams. By the end of the 1948 season, there were over 20 African American players on NFL rosters, a significant increase from just a few years earlier.

The year 1948 was another important year in the history of the NFL. The merger with the AAFC helped to solidify the league's position as the premier professional football league in the United States. The championship game was a hard-fought battle that showcased the best of what the NFL had to offer. And the continued progress towards greater racial integration helped to make the NFL a more inclusive and diverse league. Overall, 1948 was a year of continued growth and progress for the NFL.

1949

The year 1949 was a momentous one for the NFL. It was a year of expansion, innovation, and continued progress towards greater equality and diversity.

Expansion

The NFL continued to expand in 1949, with the addition of three new teams: the New York Bulldogs, the Chicago Hornets, and the Green Bay Packers. The Packers, who had previously been a part of the rival All-America Football Conference (AAFC), joined the NFL as part of the league's merger with the AAFC.

The Bulldogs and Hornets were both short-lived teams, lasting only one season in the NFL before folding. The Packers, on the other hand, would go on to become one of the most successful teams in NFL history, winning multiple championships and establishing themselves as one of the league's premier franchises.

Innovation

The 1949 season also saw a number of innovations in the NFL. The league introduced the first-ever televised game, a matchup between the Philadelphia Eagles and the Brooklyn Dodgers on October 22, 1949. The game was broadcast on a local Philadelphia television station and was a huge success, paving the way for the NFL's eventual domination of television in the decades to come.

The 1949 season also saw the introduction of a new rule that required players to wear helmets with chinstraps. This was an important safety measure that helped to reduce the number of head injuries and concussions in the NFL.

The Championship Game

The 1949 NFL Championship Game featured the Philadelphia Eagles against the Los Angeles Rams. The game was played on December 18, 1949, at the Los Angeles Memorial Coliseum. The Rams won the game 24-14, thanks in large part to a dominant performance by quarterback Bob Waterfield.

Waterfield threw for 298 yards and two touchdowns, leading the Rams to their first-ever NFL championship. The Eagles, led by quarterback Tommy Thompson and running back Steve Van Buren, put up a strong fight but were ultimately unable to overcome the Rams' high-powered offense.

Integration

In 1949, the NFL continued to make progress towards greater racial integration. The Detroit Lions signed an African American player named Bob Mann, who would go on to become one of the team's top receivers. Mann's success helped to further open the door for other African American players to be signed by NFL teams.

By the end of the 1949 season, there were over 30 African American players on NFL rosters, a significant increase from just a few years earlier. This progress towards greater equality and diversity would continue in the years to come, paving the way for a more inclusive and dynamic NFL.

Conclusion

The year 1949 was an important year in the history of the NFL. The addition of three new teams, the introduction of televised games and helmet safety rules, and the dominant performance of the Los Angeles Rams in the championship game all helped to solidify the NFL's position as the premier professional football league in the United States.

And the continued progress towards greater racial integration and diversity helped to make the NFL a more dynamic and inclusive league, setting the stage for the exciting developments and innovations that would come in the decades to come. Overall, 1949 was a year of expansion, innovation, and progress for the NFL.

THE 1950'S

1950

The year 1950 was an exciting time for the NFL. The league was growing in popularity, with more and more fans tuning in to watch their favorite teams battle it out on the gridiron. Let's take a closer look at the NFL in 1950, examining some of the key events, players, and teams that made the season one to remember.

The Teams of 1950

In 1950, the NFL consisted of 13 teams, split into two conferences: the National Conference and the American Conference. The National Conference was made up of the Chicago Bears, Detroit Lions, Green Bay Packers, Los Angeles Rams, New York Giants, and San Francisco 49ers. The American Conference consisted of the Baltimore Colts, Chicago Cardinals, Cleveland Browns, New York Yanks, Philadelphia Eagles, Pittsburgh Steelers, and Washington Redskins.

One of the most dominant teams of the era was the Cleveland Browns. Led by quarterback Otto Graham, the Browns won the NFL championship in both 1948 and 1949 and were poised for another strong season in 1950. Other strong teams included the Los Angeles Rams, who had won the NFL championship in 1949, and the Chicago Bears, who had won the championship in 1946 and 1947.

The Players of 1950

The NFL in 1950 featured some of the most talented players in league history. One of the most notable was quarterback Otto Graham of the Cleveland Browns. Graham was known for his accuracy and leadership on the field, and he led the Browns to three consecutive NFL championships from 1950 to 1952.

Other notable players included running back Steve Van Buren of the Philadelphia Eagles, who had led the league in rushing yards in both 1947 and 1949, and defensive end Doug Atkins of the Cleveland Browns, who would go on to be inducted into the Pro Football Hall of Fame.

The Season of 1950

The 1950 NFL season kicked off on September 16, 1950, with the Cleveland Browns taking on the Philadelphia Eagles. The Browns would go on to win the game 35-10, setting the tone for what would be another dominant season.

Throughout the season, the Browns continued to impress, winning their first 10 games and finishing the regular season with a record of 10-2. The Los Angeles Rams also had a strong season, finishing with a record of 9-3 and earning a spot in the NFL championship game.

On December 24, 1950, the Cleveland Browns and the Los Angeles Rams faced off in the NFL championship game at the Los Angeles Memorial Coliseum. The game was a hard-fought battle, with both teams playing tough defense and trading touchdowns throughout the game. In the end, it was the Cleveland Browns who emerged victorious, winning the game 30-28 and claiming their third consecutive NFL championship.

The NFL in 1950 was a season to remember, with the Cleveland Browns dominating the league and winning their third consecutive NFL championship. The season featured some of the most talented players in league history, and the league continued to grow in popularity and gain new fans.

As we move forward in time, the NFL will continue to evolve and change, but the memories of the 1950 season will always hold a special place in the hearts of football fans.

1951

The NFL in 1951 was a league on the rise. It was a time when the league was beginning to expand, as new teams were being added and rivalries were beginning to develop. The year 1951 was also significant for the league in terms of the players and teams that were dominating the league.

Teams

In 1951, the NFL consisted of 12 teams, which were divided into two divisions: the American Conference and the National Conference. The American Conference comprised of the Baltimore Colts, the Chicago Bears, the Los Angeles Rams, the New York Giants, the Philadelphia Eagles, and the Washington Redskins. The National Conference comprised of the Chicago Cardinals, the Cleveland Browns, the Detroit Lions, the Green Bay Packers, the New York Yanks, and the Pittsburgh Steelers.

The dominant teams in the NFL in 1951 were the Cleveland Browns and the Los Angeles Rams. The Browns, led by quarterback Otto Graham and coach Paul Brown, were on their way to their third straight NFL championship. The Rams, led by quarterback Norm Van Brocklin, were also having a strong season and were in contention for the championship.

Players

The players who dominated the league in 1951 included Otto Graham, who was the quarterback for the Cleveland

Browns. Graham had a remarkable season, throwing for 2,205 yards and 17 touchdowns, leading the Browns to the championship game. Other standout players included Norm Van Brocklin of the Los Angeles Rams, who threw for 2,527 yards and 12 touchdowns, and Tom Fears, who was a wide receiver for the Rams and caught 77 passes for 1,116 yards and eight touchdowns.

The State of the League

The NFL was in a period of expansion in 1951. In the years leading up to 1951, several new teams were added to the league, including the Dallas Texans, the Baltimore Colts, and the San Francisco 49ers. This expansion was a sign that the league was growing and becoming more popular.

However, the NFL was facing challenges in terms of competition from other sports leagues. In particular, the newly formed All-America Football Conference (AAFC) was competing with the NFL for fans and players. The AAFC was home to some of the best players in football, including Otto Graham, who was playing for the Cleveland Browns before they joined the NFL in 1950. The competition between the two leagues was intense, and it was unclear which league would come out on top.

The NFL in 1951 was a league on the rise, with new teams being added and rivalries beginning to develop. The dominant teams were the Cleveland Browns and the Los Angeles Rams, and the standout players included Otto Graham, Norm Van Brocklin, and Tom Fears. Despite facing competition from other sports leagues, the NFL was growing in popularity and was on its way to becoming the dominant professional football league in the United States.

1952

The NFL in 1952 was a league in transition. The league had expanded to 12 teams and was beginning to establish itself as the dominant professional football league in the United States.

Teams

In 1952, the NFL consisted of 12 teams, which were divided into two divisions: the American Conference and the National Conference. The American Conference comprised of the Baltimore Colts, the Chicago Bears, the Detroit Lions, the Green Bay Packers, the Los Angeles Rams, and the San Francisco 49ers. The National Conference comprised of the Chicago Cardinals, the Cleveland Browns, the New York Giants, the Philadelphia Eagles, the Pittsburgh Steelers, and the Washington Redskins.

The dominant teams in the NFL in 1952 were the Detroit Lions and the Cleveland Browns. The Lions, led by quarterback Bobby Layne and coach Buddy Parker, were on their way to their first NFL championship since 1935. The Browns, led by quarterback Otto Graham and coach Paul Brown, were also having a strong season and were in contention for the championship.

Players

The players who dominated the league in 1952 included Bobby Layne, who was the quarterback for the Detroit Lions. Layne had a remarkable season, throwing for 2,447 yards and 19 touchdowns, leading the Lions to the championship game. Other standout players included Otto Graham of the Cleveland Browns, who threw for 2,205 yards and 18 touchdowns, and Doak Walker, who was a running back for the Lions and rushed for 386 yards and five touchdowns.

The State of the League

The NFL in 1952 was a league in transition. The league was beginning to establish itself as the dominant professional football league in the United States, but it was still facing challenges from other sports leagues. In particular, the All-America Football Conference (AAFC) had merged with the NFL in 1950, and several of its teams, including the San Francisco 49ers and the Cleveland Browns, were still among the strongest teams in the league.

The competition between the NFL and other sports leagues was intense, but the NFL was slowly emerging as the dominant league. The league had established a strong fan base and was beginning to attract talented players from other sports leagues.

The NFL in 1952 was a league in transition, but it was beginning to establish itself as the dominant professional football league in the United States. The dominant teams were the Detroit Lions and the Cleveland Browns, and the standout players included Bobby Layne, Otto Graham, and Doak Walker. Despite facing challenges from other sports leagues, the NFL was slowly emerging as the dominant league and was on its way to becoming a cultural phenomenon in the United States.

1953

The NFL in 1953 was a league that continued to grow and evolve. The league had expanded to 12 teams and had established itself as the dominant professional football league in the United States. This section will explore the teams, players, and the state of the league during this pivotal year.

Teams

The NFL in 1953 consisted of 12 teams, divided into two divisions: the American Conference and the National Conference. The American Conference was comprised of the Baltimore Colts, the Chicago Bears, the Detroit Lions, the Green Bay Packers, the Los Angeles Rams, and the San Francisco 49ers. The National Conference included the Chicago Cardinals, the Cleveland Browns, the New York Giants, the Philadelphia Eagles, the Pittsburgh Steelers, and the Washington Redskins.

The Cleveland Browns were the dominant team in the NFL in 1953, winning their third straight championship. The Browns, led by quarterback Otto Graham and coach Paul Brown, were considered one of the greatest teams in NFL history, with a record of 11-1-0.

Players

The players who dominated the league in 1953 included Otto Graham, who was the quarterback for the Cleveland Browns. Graham had a phenomenal season, throwing for 2,318 yards and 11 touchdowns. Other standout players included Doak Walker, who was a running back for the Detroit Lions and rushed for 386 yards and four touchdowns, and Ollie Matson, who was a running back for the Chicago Cardinals and rushed for 853 yards and six touchdowns.

The State of the League

The NFL in 1953 was a league that was growing and evolving. The league had established a strong fan base and was beginning to attract talented players from other sports leagues. In particular, the league was starting to attract more players from college football, which was becoming increasingly popular in the United States.

The competition between the NFL and other sports leagues was still intense, but the NFL was beginning to establish itself as the dominant league. The league had established partnerships with major television networks, which helped to increase its visibility and popularity.

The NFL in 1953 was a league that continued to grow and evolve. The dominant team was the Cleveland Browns, and the standout players included Otto Graham, Doak Walker, and Ollie Matson. Despite facing challenges from other sports leagues, the NFL was starting to establish itself as the dominant professional football league in the United States, thanks to its strong fan base, talented players, and partnerships with major television networks.

1954

The NFL in 1954 was a league that continued to grow and evolve. The league had expanded to 12 teams and had established itself as the dominant professional football league in the United States.

Teams

The NFL in 1954 consisted of 12 teams, divided into two divisions: the American Conference and the National Conference. The American Conference included the Baltimore Colts, the Chicago Bears, the Detroit Lions, the Green Bay Packers, the Los Angeles Rams, and the San Francisco 49ers. The National Conference included the Chicago Cardinals, the Cleveland Browns, the New York Giants, the Philadelphia Eagles, the Pittsburgh Steelers, and the Washington Redskins.

The Cleveland Browns were once again the dominant team in the NFL in 1954, winning their fourth straight championship. The Browns, led by quarterback Otto

Graham and coach Paul Brown, had a record of 9-3-0 and defeated the Detroit Lions in the championship game.

Players

The players who dominated the league in 1954 included Otto Graham, who was the quarterback for the Cleveland Browns. Graham had another phenomenal season, throwing for 1,689 yards and 15 touchdowns. Other standout players included Tom Fears, who was a wide receiver for the Los Angeles Rams and caught 77 passes for 1,116 yards and six touchdowns, and Frank Gifford, who was a running back for the New York Giants and rushed for 819 yards and four touchdowns.

The State of the League

The NFL in 1954 was a league that continued to grow and evolve. The league had established a strong fan base and was becoming increasingly popular in the United States. The league had also established partnerships with major television networks, which helped to increase its visibility and popularity.

The competition between the NFL and other sports leagues remained intense, but the NFL was continuing to establish itself as the dominant league. The league was attracting more talented players from college football and was starting to attract more fans from across the country.

The NFL in 1954 was a league that continued to grow and evolve. The dominant team was the Cleveland Browns, and the standout players included Otto Graham, Tom Fears, and Frank Gifford. The NFL was establishing itself as the dominant professional football league in the United States, thanks to its strong fan base, talented players, and partnerships with major television networks.

1955

The NFL in 1955 was a league that continued to grow and evolve. The league had expanded to 12 teams and had established itself as the dominant professional football league in the United States.

Teams

The NFL in 1955 consisted of 12 teams, divided into two divisions: the American Conference and the National Conference. The American Conference included the Baltimore Colts, the Chicago Bears, the Detroit Lions, the Green Bay Packers, the Los Angeles Rams, and the San Francisco 49ers. The National Conference included the Chicago Cardinals, the Cleveland Browns, the New York Giants, the Philadelphia Eagles, the Pittsburgh Steelers, and the Washington Redskins.

The Cleveland Browns continued their dominance of the NFL in 1955, winning their fifth straight championship. The Browns, led by quarterback Otto Graham and coach Paul Brown, had a record of 9-2-1 and defeated the Los Angeles Rams in the championship game.

Players

The players who dominated the league in 1955 included Otto Graham, who was the quarterback for the Cleveland Browns. Graham had another outstanding season, throwing for 2,205 yards and 17 touchdowns. Other standout players included Harlon Hill, who was a wide receiver for the Chicago Bears and caught 47 passes for 1,128 yards and 11 touchdowns, and Alan Ameche, who was a running back for the Baltimore Colts and rushed for 961 yards and nine touchdowns.

The State of the League

The NFL in 1955 was a league that continued to grow and evolve. The league had established a strong fan base and was becoming increasingly popular in the United States. The league had also established partnerships with major television networks, which helped to increase its visibility and popularity.

The competition between the NFL and other sports leagues remained intense, but the NFL was continuing to establish itself as the dominant league. The league was attracting more talented players from college football and was starting to attract more fans from across the country.

The NFL in 1955 was a league that continued to grow and evolve. The dominant team was the Cleveland Browns, and the standout players included Otto Graham, Harlon Hill, and Alan Ameche. The NFL was establishing itself as the dominant professional football league in the United States, thanks to its strong fan base, talented players, and partnerships with major television networks.

1956

The NFL in 1956 was a league that continued to grow and evolve. The league had expanded to 12 teams and had established itself as the dominant professional football league in the United States.

Teams

The NFL in 1956 consisted of 12 teams, divided into two divisions: the Eastern Conference and the Western Conference. The Eastern Conference included the Cleveland Browns, the New York Giants, the Philadelphia Eagles, the Pittsburgh Steelers, the Washington Redskins, and the Chicago Cardinals. The Western Conference included the Baltimore Colts, the Chicago Bears, the Detroit Lions, the Green Bay Packers, the Los Angeles Rams, and the San Francisco 49ers.

The New York Giants won the Eastern Conference with a record of 8-3-1, while the Chicago Bears won the Western Conference with a record of 9-2-1. The Giants and Bears faced off in the championship game, which was held at Yankee Stadium in New York. The Giants won the game 47-7, earning their first championship since 1938.

Players

The players who dominated the league in 1956 included Johnny Unitas, who was the quarterback for the Baltimore Colts. Unitas had an outstanding season, throwing for 2,550 yards and 19 touchdowns. Other standout players included Frank Gifford, who was a running back for the New York Giants and rushed for 819 yards and five touchdowns, and Lenny Moore, who was a running back for the Baltimore Colts and rushed for 598 yards and nine touchdowns.

The State of the League

The NFL in 1956 was a league that continued to grow and evolve. The league had established a strong fan base and was becoming increasingly popular in the United States. The league had also established partnerships with major television networks, which helped to increase its visibility and popularity.

The competition between the NFL and other sports leagues remained intense, but the NFL was continuing to establish itself as the dominant league. The league was attracting more talented players from college football and was starting to attract more fans from across the country.

The NFL in 1956 was a league that continued to grow and evolve. The New York Giants won their first championship since 1938, and the standout players included Johnny Unitas, Frank Gifford, and Lenny Moore. The NFL was establishing itself as the dominant professional football league in the United States, thanks to its strong fan base, talented players, and partnerships with major television networks.

1957

The NFL in 1957 was a league that continued to grow and evolve. The league had expanded to 12 teams and had established itself as the dominant professional football league in the United States.

Teams

The NFL in 1957 consisted of 12 teams, divided into two divisions: the Eastern Conference and the Western Conference. The Eastern Conference included the Cleveland Browns, the New York Giants, the Philadelphia Eagles, the Pittsburgh Steelers, the Washington Redskins, and the Chicago Cardinals. The Western Conference included the Baltimore Colts, the Chicago Bears, the Detroit Lions, the Green Bay Packers, the Los Angeles Rams, and the San Francisco 49ers.

The Detroit Lions won the Western Conference with a record of 8-4, while the Cleveland Browns won the Eastern Conference with a record of 9-2-1. The Browns and Lions faced off in the championship game, which was held at Briggs Stadium in Detroit. The Lions won the game 59-14, earning their third championship in six years.

Players

The players who dominated the league in 1957 included Jim Brown, who was a running back for the Cleveland Browns. Brown had an outstanding season, rushing for 1,527 yards and 17 touchdowns. Other standout players included Paul Hornung, who was a running back for the Green Bay Packers and rushed for 597 yards and five touchdowns, and Raymond Berry, who was a wide receiver for the Baltimore Colts and caught 47 passes for 757 yards and five touchdowns.

The State of the League

The NFL in 1957 was a league that continued to grow and evolve. The league had established a strong fan base and was becoming increasingly popular in the United States. The league had also established partnerships with major television networks, which helped to increase its visibility and popularity.

The competition between the NFL and other sports leagues remained intense, but the NFL was continuing to establish itself as the dominant league. The league was attracting more talented players from college football and was starting to attract more fans from across the country.

The NFL in 1957 was a league that continued to grow and evolve. The Detroit Lions won their third championship in six years, and the standout players included Jim Brown, Paul Hornung, and Raymond Berry. The NFL was establishing itself as the dominant professional football league in the United States, thanks to its strong fan base, talented players, and partnerships with major television networks.

1958

The NFL in 1958 was a season marked by intense competition, thrilling games, and heartbreaking losses.

Teams

The NFL in 1958 consisted of 12 teams, divided into two divisions: the Eastern Conference and the Western Conference. The Eastern Conference included the Cleveland Browns, the New York Giants, the Philadelphia Eagles, the Pittsburgh Steelers, the Washington Redskins, and the Chicago Cardinals. The Western Conference included the Baltimore Colts, the Chicago Bears, the Detroit Lions, the Green Bay Packers, the Los Angeles Rams, and the San Francisco 49ers.

The Baltimore Colts, led by quarterback Johnny Unitas, won the Western Conference with a record of 9-3, while the New York Giants won the Eastern Conference with a record of 9-3. The Colts and Giants faced off in the championship game, which was held at Yankee Stadium in New York City. The game became known as "The Greatest Game Ever Played" and ended in a thrilling 23-17 victory for the Colts in overtime, earning them their first NFL championship.

Players

The players who dominated the league in 1958 included Johnny Unitas, who threw for 2,007 yards and 19 touchdowns, and Jim Brown, who rushed for 1,527 yards and 17 touchdowns. Other standout players included Raymond Berry, who caught 56 passes for 794 yards and five touchdowns, and Alan Ameche, who rushed for 961 yards and nine touchdowns.

The State of the League

The NFL in 1958 was a league that continued to grow and evolve. The league had established itself as the dominant professional football league in the United States and was attracting more talented players from college football. The league's partnerships with major television networks helped to increase its visibility and popularity.

The competition between the NFL and other sports leagues remained intense, but the NFL was continuing to establish itself as the premier league. The league was attracting more fans from across the country, and the popularity of the game was spreading to new regions.

The NFL in 1958 was a season marked by intense competition, thrilling games, and heartbreaking losses. The Baltimore Colts, led by Johnny Unitas, won their first championship in a thrilling overtime victory over the New York Giants. The standout players included Johnny Unitas, Jim Brown, Raymond Berry, and Alan Ameche. The NFL was continuing to establish itself as the dominant professional football league in the United States and was attracting more fans and talented players every year.

1959

The NFL in 1959 was a season filled with surprises, upsets, and breakthrough performances.

Teams

The NFL in 1959 consisted of 12 teams, divided into two divisions: the Eastern Conference and the Western Conference. The Eastern Conference included the Cleveland Browns, the New York Giants, the Philadelphia Eagles, the Pittsburgh Steelers, the Washington Redskins, and the Chicago Cardinals. The Western Conference included the Baltimore Colts, the Chicago Bears, the

Detroit Lions, the Green Bay Packers, the Los Angeles Rams, and the San Francisco 49ers.

The Baltimore Colts, led by quarterback Johnny Unitas, won the Western Conference with a record of 9-3, while the New York Giants won the Eastern Conference with a record of 10-2. The Colts and Giants faced off in the championship game, which was held at Memorial Stadium in Baltimore. The Colts won the game 31-16, earning their second NFL championship.

Players

The players who dominated the league in 1959 included Johnny Unitas, who threw for 2,899 yards and 32 touchdowns, and Jim Brown, who rushed for 1,329 yards and 14 touchdowns. Other standout players included Raymond Berry, who caught 66 passes for 966 yards and nine touchdowns, and Bobby Mitchell, who caught 58 passes for 1,168 yards and nine touchdowns.

The State of the League

The NFL in 1959 was a league that was continuing to evolve and grow. The league's popularity was spreading beyond traditional football markets, and more and more people were tuning in to watch the games on television. The league was also expanding its reach globally, with the first NFL game played outside of North America taking place in Toronto, Canada.

The competition between the NFL and other sports leagues remained intense, but the NFL was continuing to establish itself as the premier professional football league in the United States. The league's partnerships with major television networks were helping to increase its visibility and popularity, and more and more companies were seeking to sponsor and advertise during NFL games.

The NFL in 1959 was a season marked by breakthrough performances, surprising upsets, and thrilling games. The Baltimore Colts, led by Johnny Unitas, won their second championship in a dominant performance over the New York Giants. The standout players included Johnny Unitas, Jim Brown, Raymond Berry, and Bobby Mitchell. The NFL was continuing to evolve and grow, expanding its reach globally and establishing itself as the premier professional football league in the United States.

THE 1960'S

1960

The NFL in 1960 was a season of transition, as new teams entered the league and a new era of football was beginning to emerge.

Teams

The NFL in 1960 consisted of 13 teams, divided into two conferences: the Eastern Conference and the Western Conference. The Eastern Conference included the Cleveland Browns, the New York Giants, the Philadelphia Eagles, the Pittsburgh Steelers, and the Washington Redskins. The Western Conference included the Baltimore Colts, the Chicago Bears, the Dallas Cowboys, the Detroit Lions, the Green Bay Packers, the Los Angeles Rams, the St. Louis Cardinals, and the San Francisco 49ers.

The Dallas Cowboys were a new expansion team in the NFL, and they were the first team to join the league since the Cleveland Browns in 1950. The Cowboys struggled in their first season, finishing with a record of 0-11-1. The Philadelphia Eagles won the Eastern Conference with a record of 10-2, while the Green Bay Packers won the Western Conference with a record of 8-4.

Players

The players who dominated the league in 1960 included Johnny Unitas, who threw for 2,621 yards and 24 touchdowns, and Jim Brown, who rushed for 1,257 yards and nine touchdowns. Other standout players included Paul Hornung, who scored 146 points and rushed for 671 yards, and Raymond Berry, who caught 74 passes for 1,298 yards and 10 touchdowns.

The State of the League

The NFL in 1960 was a league that was continuing to evolve and grow. The addition of the Dallas Cowboys brought the league's total number of teams to 13, and the league was continuing to expand its reach beyond traditional football markets. The league's partnerships with major television networks were helping to increase its visibility and popularity, and more and more companies were seeking to sponsor and advertise during NFL games.

The competition between the NFL and other sports leagues remained intense, but the NFL was continuing to establish itself as the premier professional football league in the United States. The league was also continuing to implement new rules and regulations aimed at making the game safer and more entertaining for players and fans alike.

The NFL in 1960 was a season of transition, as the league was continuing to evolve and grow. The addition of the Dallas Cowboys brought the league's total number of teams to 13, and the league was continuing to expand its reach beyond traditional football markets. The standout players included Johnny Unitas, Jim Brown, Paul Hornung, and Raymond Berry. The NFL was continuing to establish itself as the premier professional football league in the United States, implementing new rules and regulations aimed at making the game safer and more entertaining for players and fans alike.

1961

The NFL in 1961 was a season marked by dominant teams, legendary players, and groundbreaking moments.

Teams

The NFL in 1961 consisted of 14 teams, divided into two conferences: the Eastern Conference and the Western Conference. The Eastern Conference included the Cleveland Browns, the New York Giants, the Philadelphia Eagles, the Pittsburgh Steelers, and the St. Louis Cardinals. The Western Conference included the Baltimore Colts, the Chicago Bears, the Dallas Cowboys, the Detroit Lions, the Green Bay Packers, the Los Angeles Rams, the Minnesota Vikings, the San Francisco 49ers, and the newly-added Atlanta Falcons.

Players

The players who dominated the league in 1961 included Jim Brown, who rushed for a league-leading 1,408 yards and 15 touchdowns, and Johnny Unitas, who threw for 2,824 yards and 19 touchdowns. Other standout players included Paul Hornung, who scored 146 points and rushed for 671 yards, and Fran Tarkenton, who led the expansion Atlanta Falcons with 1,997 passing yards and 18 touchdowns.

The State of the League

The NFL in 1961 was a league that was on the rise, with increasing popularity and attention from fans and media. The league's partnerships with major television networks continued to bring the game into more homes across the country, and the league's expansion to include the Atlanta Falcons marked a significant step in the league's growth.

The competition between the NFL and other sports leagues remained intense, with the newly-formed American Football League (AFL) challenging the NFL for players and viewers. However, the NFL remained the dominant force in professional football, with a reputation for a higher level of play and more established teams.

Groundbreaking Moments

The 1961 NFL season was also marked by several groundbreaking moments that would go on to shape the future of the league. One such moment was the debut of the first-ever Monday Night Football game on September 11, featuring the New York Giants and the St. Louis Cardinals. The game was a success, and Monday Night Football would go on to become a staple of the NFL's weekly schedule.

Another significant moment came on November 27, when the Chicago Bears defeated the New York Giants 17-14 in the first-ever televised NFL game in color. The use of color television would become more widespread in the coming years, leading to a more vivid and engaging viewing experience for fans.

The NFL in 1961 was a season of dominance, with standout teams and players making their mark on the league. The addition of the Atlanta Falcons marked a significant step in the league's expansion, while the debut of Monday Night Football and the use of color television set the stage for future innovations. The NFL remained the dominant force in professional football, with increasing popularity and attention from fans and media alike.

1962

The NFL in 1962 was a season of change, with new teams, new stars, and new rules.

Teams

The NFL in 1962 consisted of 14 teams, divided into two conferences: the Eastern Conference and the Western Conference. The Eastern Conference included the

Cleveland Browns, the Dallas Cowboys, the New York Giants, the Philadelphia Eagles, Pittsburgh Steelers, and the St. Louis Cardinals. The Western Conference included the Baltimore Colts, the Chicago Bears, the Detroit Lions, the Green Bay Packers, the Los Angeles Rams, the Minnesota Vikings, the San Francisco 49ers, and the expansion team, the Houston Oilers.

Players

The players who dominated the league in 1962 included Jim Brown, who rushed for 1,863 yards and scored 18 touchdowns, and Johnny Unitas, who threw for 2,824 yards and 19 touchdowns. Other standout players included Y.A. Tittle, who threw for 3,224 yards and 33 touchdowns, and Bobby Mitchell, who led the league with 72 receptions for 1,384 yards and 11 touchdowns.

Major Events

The NFL in 1962 was a season marked by several major events that would go on to shape the future of the league. One such event was the expansion of the league to include the Houston Oilers, the first team to be added to the NFL since 1952. The addition of the Oilers gave the league a presence in the growing Southern market and laid the foundation for further expansion in the future.

Another significant event was the introduction of several new rules, including the elimination of the two-way player rule, which had required players to play on both offense and defense. This change allowed players to specialize in one position, leading to an increase in the level of play and the emergence of new stars.

The State of the League

The NFL in 1962 was a league in transition, with increasing popularity and attention from fans and media. The league's partnerships with major television networks continued to bring the game into more homes across the country, and the introduction of new rules and new teams signaled the league's commitment to innovation and growth.

Competition between the NFL and other sports leagues remained intense, with the newly-formed American Football League (AFL) challenging the NFL for players and viewers. However, the NFL remained the dominant force in professional football, with a reputation for a higher level of play and more established teams.

The NFL in 1962 was a season of change, with new teams, new stars, and new rules shaping the future of the league. The addition of the Houston Oilers and the elimination of the two-way player rule laid the foundation for further expansion and innovation in the coming years. The NFL remained the dominant force in professional football, with increasing popularity and attention from fans and media alike.

1963

The NFL in 1963 was a year marked by tragedy, as well as triumphs on and off the field. Let's explore the teams, players, and major events that shaped the league during this tumultuous year.

Teams

The NFL in 1963 consisted of 14 teams, divided into two conferences: the Eastern Conference and the Western Conference. The Eastern Conference included the Cleveland Browns, the Dallas Cowboys, the New York

Giants, the Philadelphia Eagles, Pittsburgh Steelers, and the St. Louis Cardinals. The Western Conference included the Baltimore Colts, the Chicago Bears, the Detroit Lions, the Green Bay Packers, the Los Angeles Rams, the Minnesota Vikings, the San Francisco 49ers, and the expansion team, the Dallas Texans.

Players

The players who dominated the league in 1963 included Jim Brown, who rushed for 1,863 yards and scored 15 touchdowns, and Johnny Unitas, who threw for 3,481 yards and 26 touchdowns. Other standout players included Sonny Jurgensen, who threw for 3,723 yards and 32 touchdowns, and Tommy McDonald, who led the league with 67 receptions for 1,228 yards and 13 touchdowns.

Major Events

The NFL in 1963 was a season marked by tragedy, as well as triumphs on and off the field. One of the most significant events was the assassination of President John F. Kennedy on November 22, 1963, which cast a pall over the entire country and left many questioning whether or not the NFL games scheduled for that weekend should be played. After consulting with the Kennedy family, the NFL commissioner Pete Rozelle decided to play the games as scheduled, a decision that was widely criticized at the time.

On the field, the NFL in 1963 saw the Dallas Cowboys win their first ever Western Conference Championship, behind the leadership of quarterback Don Meredith and the "Doomsday Defense" anchored by Bob Lilly and Lee Roy Jordan. In the Eastern Conference, the New York Giants finished with the best record, led by quarterback Y.A. Tittle, who threw for 3,145 yards and 36 touchdowns.

The State of the League

The NFL in 1963 was a league still in transition, with increasing popularity and attention from fans and media. The league continued to expand, with the addition of the Dallas Texans, who would eventually become the Kansas City Chiefs. The NFL also saw increased competition from the upstart American Football League (AFL), which was gaining a foothold in new markets and signing top talent away from the NFL.

The NFL in 1963 was a year marked by tragedy and triumphs on and off the field. The assassination of President Kennedy cast a shadow over the entire country, and the decision to play NFL games that weekend was controversial. However, the league continued to grow in popularity and expand, with new teams and new talent emerging every year. The NFL remained the dominant force in professional football, but the challenges posed by the AFL meant that the league would have to continue to evolve and adapt to stay ahead of the competition.

1964

The year 1964 was a significant one in the history of the NFL. It marked the 45th season of the league's existence, and several notable events occurred during the year.

Teams

In 1964, the NFL consisted of 14 teams, divided into two conferences: the Eastern Conference and the Western Conference. The Eastern Conference comprised the Cleveland Browns, Dallas Cowboys, New York Giants, Philadelphia Eagles, Pittsburgh Steelers, St. Louis Cardinals, and Washington Redskins. The Western Conference was made up of the Baltimore Colts, Chicago

Bears, Detroit Lions, Green Bay Packers, Los Angeles Rams, Minnesota Vikings, and San Francisco 49ers.

Players

Several notable players were active in the NFL in 1964. One of the most prominent was Jim Brown, the star running back for the Cleveland Browns. Brown had already established himself as one of the best players in the league and was coming off a season in which he rushed for 1,446 yards and 7 touchdowns. Other notable players included Johnny Unitas, the quarterback for the Baltimore Colts, and Bart Starr, the quarterback for the Green Bay Packers.

Events

The 1964 NFL season was full of exciting games and memorable moments. One of the most significant events of the season was the championship game between the Cleveland Browns and the Baltimore Colts. The game was played on December 27, 1964, in Cleveland, and was dubbed the "Greatest Game Ever Played" by many fans and analysts.

The game was a back-and-forth affair, with both teams exchanging leads throughout the contest. In the fourth quarter, the Colts took a 27-21 lead, but the Browns responded with a touchdown to tie the game at 27-27. The game went into overtime, and the Colts eventually won 31-27 on a touchdown run by Alan Ameche.

Another memorable moment from the 1964 NFL season was the emergence of the Dallas Cowboys. The Cowboys had been a struggling expansion team since joining the league in 1960, but in 1964, they had their first winning season, finishing with a record of 5-8-1. The Cowboys' success was due in large part to the outstanding play of quarterback Don Meredith, who threw for 2,805 yards and 24 touchdowns.

The 1964 NFL season was a significant one in the league's history, featuring many of the game's greatest players and memorable moments. The championship game between the Cleveland Browns and the Baltimore Colts was a classic, and the emergence of the Dallas Cowboys as a competitive team was a sign of things to come. Overall, the 1964 NFL season was a fitting tribute to the league's first 45 years, and it set the stage for even more exciting seasons to come.

1965

The year 1965 marked the 46th season of the NFL, and it was a year of change and transition for the league.

Teams

In 1965, the NFL consisted of 14 teams, divided into two conferences: the Eastern Conference and the Western Conference. The Eastern Conference comprised the Cleveland Browns, Dallas Cowboys, New York Giants, Philadelphia Eagles, Pittsburgh Steelers, St. Louis Cardinals, and Washington Redskins. The Western Conference was made up of the Baltimore Colts, Chicago Bears, Detroit Lions, Green Bay Packers, Los Angeles Rams, Minnesota Vikings, and San Francisco 49ers.

Players

Several notable players were active in the NFL in 1965. Jim Brown, the star running back for the Cleveland Browns, had another outstanding season, rushing for 1,544 yards and 17 touchdowns. Johnny Unitas, the quarterback for the Baltimore Colts, continued to be one of the best quarterbacks in the league, throwing for 2,482 yards and 23 touchdowns. Other notable players included Bart Starr, the quarterback for the Green Bay Packers, and Gale Sayers, the running back for the Chicago Bears.

Events

The 1965 NFL season was full of exciting games and memorable moments. One of the most significant events of the season was the introduction of the NFL Draft, which was held on November 28, 1964. The draft was designed to ensure that all NFL teams had an equal opportunity to acquire new talent and maintain parity within the league.

Another significant event was the relocation of the Cardinals from St. Louis to Phoenix. The team had struggled to attract fans in St. Louis and decided to move to a new city in the hope of building a larger fan base. The move was controversial and sparked a debate about the role of sports franchises in local communities.

In terms of on-field events, one of the most memorable moments of the 1965 NFL season was the performance of Gale Sayers in a game against the San Francisco 49ers. Sayers scored six touchdowns in the game, including four on kick returns, and set a new NFL record for most touchdowns in a single game. His performance cemented his status as one of the most exciting and talented players in the league.

The 1965 NFL season was a year of change and transition for the league, with the introduction of the NFL Draft and the relocation of the Cardinals to Phoenix. Despite these changes, the season was full of exciting games and memorable moments, including Jim Brown's outstanding season, the emergence of Gale Sayers as a star player, and the continued dominance of players like Johnny Unitas and Bart Starr. Overall, the 1965 NFL season was a fitting tribute to the league's first 46 years, and it set the stage for even more exciting seasons to come.

1966 – The birth of the Super Bowl

The year 1966 marked the 47th season of the NFL, and it was a year of both continuity and change for the league.

Teams

In 1966, the NFL consisted of 15 teams, divided into two conferences: the Eastern Conference and the Western Conference. The Eastern Conference comprised the Cleveland Browns, Dallas Cowboys, New York Giants, Philadelphia Eagles, Pittsburgh Steelers, and Washington Redskins. The Western Conference was made up of the Baltimore Colts, Chicago Bears, Detroit Lions, Green Bay Packers, Los Angeles Rams, Minnesota Vikings, San Francisco 49ers, Atlanta Falcons, and New Orleans Saints. The addition of the Falcons and the Saints expanded the NFL into the Southeastern United States, and marked the first time the league had expanded since 1950.

Players

Several notable players were active in the NFL in 1966. Jim Brown, the star running back for the Cleveland Browns, had another outstanding season, rushing for 1,544 yards and seven touchdowns. Bart Starr, the quarterback for the Green Bay Packers, continued to lead his team to success, throwing for 2,257 yards and 14 touchdowns. Other notable players included Johnny Unitas, the quarterback for the Baltimore Colts, and Gale Sayers, the running back for the Chicago Bears.

Super Bowl I

Super Bowl I, also known as the First AFL-NFL World Championship Game, was a historic event that took place on January 15, 1967, at the Los Angeles Memorial Coliseum in Los Angeles, California. It was the first-ever championship game between the National Football League (NFL) and the American Football League (AFL), which were two separate leagues at the time. The game was a culmination of a merger agreement between the two leagues, and it marked the beginning of a new era in professional football.

The first Super Bowl was a highly anticipated event, but it did not receive the same level of media coverage and hype that it does today. There were no elaborate pre-game shows, halftime shows, or even a formal name for the event. It was simply known as the AFL-NFL World Championship Game, and it was broadcasted on both NBC and CBS, with each network using its own commentators.

The game featured the NFL champion Green Bay Packers and the AFL champion Kansas City Chiefs. The Packers were led by head coach Vince Lombardi and quarterback Bart Starr, who had won three NFL championships in the previous five years. The Chiefs were coached by Hank Stram and had a potent offense led by quarterback Len Dawson and wide receiver Otis Taylor.

The game got off to a slow start, with both teams struggling to move the ball in the first quarter. However, the Packers broke the deadlock in the second quarter with a 37-yard touchdown pass from Starr to wide receiver Max McGee. The Chiefs responded with a field goal, but the Packers quickly struck back with another touchdown pass from Starr, this time to Boyd Dowler. The Packers went into halftime with a 14-10 lead.

In the second half, the Packers took control of the game, thanks in part to their dominant defense, which intercepted Dawson twice and sacked him six times. The Packers also scored two more touchdowns, one on a one-yard run by Elijah Pitts and another on a 13-yard pass from Starr to McGee. The Chiefs managed to score one more touchdown late in the game, but it was too little, too late. The final score was 35-10 in favor of the Packers.

The game was a resounding success, drawing a crowd of 61,946 and a television audience of over 50 million viewers. It marked the beginning of a new era in professional football, with the AFL and NFL agreeing to merge into one league the following year. The Super Bowl would become an annual event, growing in popularity and becoming one of the most-watched television programs in the United States.

Super Bowl I was a historic event that brought together the best teams from the NFL and AFL. It marked the beginning of a new era in professional football and set the stage for what would become one of the most-watched television events in the United States. The game was a resounding success, and it remains a significant milestone in the history of football.

Merger negotiations

Another significant event was the merger negotiations between the NFL and the AFL. The two leagues had been competing for fans and players for years, and there was growing pressure to merge in order to create a stronger, more unified professional football league. The negotiations were not finalized until 1970, but the talks that took place in 1966 set the stage for the eventual merger.

In terms of on-field events, one of the most memorable moments of the 1966 NFL season was the emergence of the Dallas Cowboys as a serious contender. The team had struggled in its early years, but in 1966, the Cowboys won their first ever playoff game, beating the Cleveland Browns 31-20 in the NFL Championship Game. Although they lost to the Packers in the first Super Bowl, the Cowboys had established themselves as a force to be reckoned with in the NFL.

The 1966 NFL season was a year of both continuity and change for the league, with the addition of two new teams and the emergence of the Dallas Cowboys as a serious contender. The season also saw the first Super Bowl, which would go on to become one of the most popular and lucrative sporting events in the world. But perhaps most importantly, the 1966 season laid the groundwork for the eventual merger of the NFL and the AFL, which would transform the sport of football and create the modern NFL as we know it today.

1967

The year 1967 was a historic one for the NFL, as it marked the league's 48th season and saw several significant events take place.

Teams

In 1967, the NFL consisted of 16 teams, divided into two conferences: the Eastern Conference and the Western Conference. The Eastern Conference comprised the Cleveland Browns, Dallas Cowboys, New York Giants, Philadelphia Eagles, Pittsburgh Steelers, and Washington Redskins. The Western Conference was made up of the Baltimore Colts, Chicago Bears, Detroit Lions, Green Bay Packers, Los Angeles Rams, Minnesota Vikings, San

Francisco 49ers, Atlanta Falcons, and New Orleans Saints. The addition of the Saints in 1967 expanded the NFL into the Southern United States, and marked the second time the league had expanded in three years.

Players

Several notable players were active in the NFL in 1967. Jim Brown, the star running back for the Cleveland Browns, had another impressive season, rushing for 1,544 yards and 17 touchdowns. Bart Starr, the quarterback for the Green Bay Packers, continued to lead his team to success, throwing for 2,096 yards and 16 touchdowns. Other notable players included Johnny Unitas, the quarterback for the Baltimore Colts, and Joe Namath, the quarterback for the New York Jets of the rival American Football League (AFL).

Events

The 1967 NFL season was full of exciting games and memorable moments. One of the most significant events of the season was the Ice Bowl, which was played on December 31, 1967, between the Dallas Cowboys and the Green Bay Packers. The game was played in brutally cold conditions, with temperatures dropping to -13 degrees Fahrenheit, and was one of the most memorable games in NFL history. The Packers won the game 21-17, thanks in part to a quarterback sneak by Bart Starr on the final play of the game.

Another significant event was the expansion of the league's playoffs, from two teams per conference to four. This meant that eight teams would compete in the playoffs, with the winners of the two conference championship games meeting in the NFL Championship Game. The Green Bay Packers won the Western Conference, while the Cleveland

Browns won the Eastern Conference. The Packers defeated the Browns in the NFL Championship Game, winning 21-17 and earning a spot in Super Bowl II.

Super Bowl II

Super Bowl II was the second championship game between the National Football League (NFL) and the American Football League (AFL), played on January 14, 1968, at the Orange Bowl in Miami, Florida. The game was a rematch of Super Bowl I, with the Green Bay Packers once again facing off against the AFL champion, this time, the Oakland Raiders.

The Packers were the defending champions and had won the first-ever Super Bowl against the Kansas City Chiefs. They were led by legendary coach Vince Lombardi and quarterback Bart Starr, who had already won two NFL championships and one Super Bowl. The Raiders, on the other hand, were making their first appearance in the Super Bowl and were led by head coach John Rauch and quarterback Daryle Lamonica.

The game started with a slow pace, with both teams struggling to score in the first quarter. However, the Packers broke the deadlock in the second quarter with a one-yard touchdown run by fullback Donny Anderson. The Raiders answered with a field goal, but the Packers came back with another touchdown, this time a 62-yard pass from Starr to wide receiver Boyd Dowler. The Packers led 13-3 at halftime.

In the second half, the Packers dominated the game, scoring three more touchdowns, one by Elijah Pitts and two by Jim Grabowski. The Raiders managed to score one more touchdown, but it was not enough, and the Packers won the game 33-14.

Bart Starr was named the game's Most Valuable Player (MVP) for the second time in a row, completing 13 out of 24 passes for 202 yards and one touchdown. The Packers' defense was also impressive, intercepting three of Lamonica's passes and holding the Raiders to only 14 points.

The game marked the end of an era for the Packers, as Vince Lombardi announced his retirement after the game. Lombardi had led the Packers to five NFL championships and two Super Bowl victories in his nine-year tenure as head coach.

Super Bowl II was not as historic as the first Super Bowl, but it was still a significant event in the history of professional football. It cemented the Packers' status as one of the greatest teams in NFL history, and it showcased the talents of future Hall of Famers like Starr, Paul Hornung, and Ray Nitschke.

In conclusion, Super Bowl II was a dominant performance by the Green Bay Packers, who secured their second consecutive championship and established themselves as one of the greatest teams in NFL history. It marked the end of an era for the Packers, as Vince Lombardi retired after the game, but it also set the stage for more exciting Super Bowls to come.

The 1967 NFL season was a historic one, with the addition of the New Orleans Saints and the expansion of the playoffs to four teams per conference. The season also saw the Ice Bowl, one of the most memorable games in NFL history, and the second Super Bowl, which marked the end of the NFL's second decade. The season was also notable for the continued dominance of the Green Bay Packers, who won their second consecutive Super Bowl and solidified their status as one of the greatest teams in NFL history.

1968

The year 1968 was another memorable one for the NFL, as the league continued to grow in popularity and expand its reach across the United States.

Teams

In 1968, the NFL consisted of 16 teams, divided into two conferences: the Eastern Conference and the Western Conference. The Eastern Conference comprised the Cleveland Browns, Dallas Cowboys, New York Giants, Philadelphia Eagles, Pittsburgh Steelers, and Washington Redskins. The Western Conference was made up of the Baltimore Colts, Chicago Bears, Detroit Lions, Green Bay Packers, Los Angeles Rams, Minnesota Vikings, San Francisco 49ers, Atlanta Falcons, and New Orleans Saints.

Players

Several notable players were active in the NFL in 1968. Running back Leroy Kelly of the Cleveland Browns had an outstanding season, rushing for 1,239 yards and 16 touchdowns. Johnny Unitas, the legendary quarterback for the Baltimore Colts, continued to play at a high level, throwing for 2,404 yards and 19 touchdowns. Other notable players included Bart Starr of the Green Bay Packers, Gale Sayers of the Chicago Bears, and Bob Hayes of the Dallas Cowboys.

Events

The 1968 NFL season was full of exciting games and memorable moments. One of the most significant events of the season was the expansion of the league to 16 teams, with the addition of the New Orleans Saints in the previous year. This marked the first time the NFL had expanded since 1961, and paved the way for further expansion in the coming years.

Another notable event was the league's first tie game since 1946, when the St. Louis Cardinals and the Philadelphia Eagles played to a 20-20 tie on November 10, 1968. This was the first tie game in the NFL in over two decades, and highlighted the importance of having a well-defined overtime rule.

The 1968 season also saw the introduction of the NFL Playoffs as we know them today. The top four teams from each conference advanced to the postseason, with the winners of the two conference championship games meeting in the NFL Championship Game. The Cleveland Browns won the Eastern Conference, while the Baltimore Colts won the Western Conference.

Super Bowl III

Super Bowl III, played on January 12, 1969, was a historic game that is often considered one of the greatest upsets in NFL history. The game was played at the Orange Bowl in Miami, Florida, and featured the Baltimore Colts, the NFL champions, and the New York Jets, the AFL champions.

The Jets were led by quarterback Joe Namath, who had guaranteed a victory for his team before the game. Namath was known for his brash and confident personality, and his guarantee was seen by many as a bold prediction that was unlikely to come true. However, Namath and the Jets were determined to prove the doubters wrong.

The game started with a slow pace, with both teams struggling to score in the first quarter. The Colts, led by legendary quarterback Johnny Unitas, were expected to dominate the game, but the Jets' defense held them to only a field goal in the first half. Meanwhile, the Jets' offense, led by Namath, scored two touchdowns, one on a one-yard run by Matt Snell and another on a 13-yard pass from Namath to George Sauer. The Jets led 14-3 at halftime.

In the second half, the Colts tried to mount a comeback, but the Jets' defense continued to stifle their offense. Namath, who had predicted victory for his team, played with confidence and poise, completing 17 of 28 passes for 206 yards and no interceptions. The Jets added a field goal in the fourth quarter, and the Colts managed to score only one more touchdown late in the game. The final score was 16-7 in favor of the Jets.

Joe Namath was named the game's Most Valuable Player (MVP) for his outstanding performance. His guarantee before the game had made him a target for criticism and skepticism, but his confidence and leadership had inspired his team to one of the greatest upsets in NFL history.

Super Bowl III was a significant event in the history of professional football. It was the first Super Bowl victory for the AFL, and it showed that the AFL could compete with the NFL. The game also helped to establish the Super Bowl as a major sporting event and one of the most-watched television programs in the United States.

Super Bowl III was a historic game that is remembered for Joe Namath's guarantee and the New York Jets' upset victory over the heavily favored Baltimore Colts. It marked a significant moment in the history of professional football and helped to establish the Super Bowl as one of the most-watched television events in the United States.

The 1968 NFL season was a historic one, with the league expanding to 16 teams and the introduction of the modern playoff system. The season also saw several notable players continue to perform at a high level, and several memorable games and events took place. The season was capped off by the NFL Championship Game, which saw the Baltimore Colts defeat the Cleveland Browns and earn a spot in Super Bowl III. Overall, the 1968 NFL season represented another step forward for the league, as it continued to grow in popularity and expand its reach across the country.

1969

The NFL in the year 1969 was a league in transition. It was the final year of the 1960s, a decade of change and turmoil in America, and the NFL was not immune to these societal shifts.

Overview of the NFL in 1969

The NFL in 1969 consisted of 16 teams, divided into two conferences: the National Football Conference (NFC) and the American Football Conference (AFC). Each conference had four divisions, with four teams in each division. The winners of each division would qualify for the playoffs, with the two conference champions meeting in the Super Bowl.

The 1969 season was the first to have four rounds of playoffs, with a wild-card team added to each conference. The Super Bowl was played in January 1970, and the AFL's Kansas City Chiefs defeated the NFL's Minnesota Vikings, 23-7.

Key Events

The NFL in 1969 was marked by several key events. In January of that year, the AFL-NFL merger was completed, with the two leagues officially becoming one entity. The new NFL consisted of 26 teams, divided into two conferences.

In August, the NFL Players Association (NFLPA) staged a strike, with players demanding higher pay and better benefits. The strike lasted for several weeks and resulted in the cancellation of one preseason game and the postponement of several regular-season games.

On the field, the NFL in 1969 saw the emergence of several legendary players. Quarterback Joe Namath led the New York Jets to their first and only Super Bowl victory, defeating the heavily favored Baltimore Colts. Running back O.J. Simpson of the Buffalo Bills became the first player in NFL history to rush for over 1,000 yards in a 14-game season. And defensive end Deacon Jones of the Los Angeles Rams coined the term "sack" to describe a tackle of the quarterback behind the line of scrimmage.

Super Bowl IV

Super Bowl IV, played on January 11, 1970, was the final championship game between the National Football League (NFL) and the American Football League (AFL), before the two leagues merged. The game was played at Tulane Stadium in New Orleans, Louisiana, and featured the AFL champion Kansas City Chiefs against the NFL champion Minnesota Vikings.

The Chiefs were led by head coach Hank Stram and quarterback Len Dawson, who had missed most of the season due to injury but returned in time for the playoffs. The Vikings, on the other hand, were led by head coach

Bud Grant and a dominant defense that had allowed the fewest points in the NFL that season.

The game started with a slow pace, with both teams struggling to score in the first quarter. However, the Chiefs broke the deadlock in the second quarter with a five-yard touchdown run by Mike Garrett. The Vikings responded with a field goal, but the Chiefs scored another touchdown before halftime, a 46-yard pass from Dawson to Otis Taylor. The Chiefs led 16-0 at halftime.

In the second half, the Chiefs continued to dominate the game, with Dawson completing 12 of 17 passes for 142 yards and one touchdown. The Vikings managed to score two touchdowns, but it was not enough, and the Chiefs won the game 23-7.

Len Dawson was named the game's Most Valuable Player (MVP) for his outstanding performance, completing 12 of 17 passes for 142 yards and one touchdown. The Chiefs' defense was also impressive, intercepting three of Joe Kapp's passes and holding the Vikings to only seven points.

Super Bowl IV was a significant event in the history of professional football, as it marked the final championship game between the NFL and the AFL before the two leagues merged. It also solidified the AFL's reputation as a legitimate professional football league, as the Chiefs' victory over the heavily favored Vikings showed that the AFL could compete with the NFL.

Super Bowl IV was a dominant performance by the Kansas City Chiefs, who secured their first-ever Super Bowl victory and established themselves as one of the best teams in the AFL. The game also marked the end of an era for professional football, as the NFL and AFL would merge the following season to form one unified league.

Trends

The NFL in 1969 was also marked by several trends that would continue to shape the league in the years to come. The passing game was becoming more prevalent, with quarterbacks such as Namath, Johnny Unitas of the Colts, and Bart Starr of the Green Bay Packers leading the way. The NFL also saw the emergence of black quarterbacks, with James Harris of the Bills and Marlin Briscoe of the Denver Broncos becoming the first African-American starting quarterbacks in league history.

Off the field, the NFL was also becoming more diverse. In 1969, the Pittsburgh Steelers hired Chuck Noll as their head coach, making him the first African-American head coach in NFL history. The league was also becoming more corporate, with television revenue and sponsorships becoming increasingly important.

The NFL in 1969 was a league in transition, marked by key events, legendary players, and emerging trends. The AFL-NFL merger and the NFLPA strike were signs of a changing landscape, while players such as Namath and Simpson helped to define the era on the field. The emergence of black quarterbacks and the hiring of Noll as the first African-American head coach were signs of a more diverse league, while the increasing importance of television revenue and sponsorships signaled a more corporate future. Overall, the NFL in 1969 was a pivotal year in the league's history, setting the stage for the decades to come.

THE 1970'S

1970

The year 1970 marked a significant moment in the history of the NFL. It was a year that saw the merger of the NFL and the American Football League (AFL), creating a new era of professional football in the United States.

The Merger

The merger between the NFL and the AFL was announced in 1966, but it wasn't until 1970 that the two leagues officially merged. The merger was a response to the growing popularity of the AFL, which had successfully challenged the dominance of the NFL in the 1960s. The merger created a single league with two conferences, the National Football Conference (NFC) and the American Football Conference (AFC), each with 13 teams.

The impact of the merger was significant. It brought about a more balanced competition between the teams, as well as an expanded television audience. The Super Bowl, which had been played since 1967 between the champions of the two leagues, became the ultimate showcase for professional football, with millions of viewers tuning in each year.

The Teams and Players

The merger also created new opportunities for players and teams. The AFL had a reputation for being more innovative and experimental in its approach to the game, and many of its teams brought with them new strategies and ideas that were quickly adopted by the NFL.

One of the most successful teams of the 1970s was the Pittsburgh Steelers, who had struggled in the 1960s but emerged as a dominant force in the AFC after the merger. Led by their "Steel Curtain" defense, the Steelers won four Super Bowls in the decade, becoming one of the most successful franchises in NFL history.

Another team that made a big impact in the 1970s was the Miami Dolphins. Led by quarterback Bob Griese and coach Don Shula, the Dolphins won two consecutive Super Bowls in 1972 and 1973, becoming the first team to have a perfect season in 1972.

Super Bowl V

Super Bowl V was played on January 17, 1971, at the Orange Bowl in Miami, Florida. The game featured the Baltimore Colts, who were making their second Super Bowl appearance, and the Dallas Cowboys, who were playing in their first Super Bowl.

The game was a closely contested affair, with both teams struggling to maintain momentum throughout the game. The Colts were led by quarterback Johnny Unitas, who had been injured for much of the season but was able to return for the playoffs. The Cowboys were led by quarterback Craig Morton and a strong defense that had allowed the fewest points in the NFC that season.

The game started with a flurry of turnovers, with the Colts and the Cowboys each giving up the ball on their first possessions. The Colts scored the first points of the game on a field goal by Jim O'Brien, but the Cowboys responded with a touchdown run by Duane Thomas to take a 7-3 lead.

In the second half, the Colts took the lead on a touchdown pass from Unitas to John Mackey. However, the Cowboys responded with a touchdown pass from Morton to Lance Rentzel to regain the lead. With less than two minutes remaining in the game, the Colts drove down the field and scored the go-ahead touchdown on a one-yard run by Tom Nowatzke. The Colts held on to win the game 16-13.

Jim O'Brien was named the game's Most Valuable Player (MVP) for his performance, which included three field goals, including the game-winning kick in the fourth quarter. The Colts' defense also played a key role, intercepting three of Morton's passes and recovering two fumbles.

Super Bowl V was a memorable game for a number of reasons. It was the first Super Bowl to be played after the AFL-NFL merger, and it featured two evenly matched teams in a closely contested game. The game was also notable for its high number of turnovers, with both teams struggling to maintain possession of the ball throughout the game.

Super Bowl V was a closely contested game that featured two evenly matched teams. The game was memorable for its high number of turnovers and its dramatic ending, with the Colts scoring the game-winning touchdown with less than two minutes remaining in the game. Jim O'Brien's game-winning field goal secured the Colts' victory and earned him the game's Most Valuable Player award.

The Evolution of the Sport

The merger also brought about changes to the game itself. The AFL had introduced a number of innovations, including the two-point conversion and the use of instant replay, which were quickly adopted by the NFL. The merger also led to the expansion of the league, with new teams being added in the 1970s and 1980s.

The 1970s also saw the emergence of a new generation of players, including quarterbacks Roger Staubach and Terry Bradshaw, and running backs O.J. Simpson and Walter Payton. These players helped to usher in a new era of football, characterized by fast-paced, high-scoring games and dynamic offenses.

The merger of the NFL and the AFL in 1970 was a turning point in the history of professional football. It created a new era of competition, innovation, and expansion, and helped to shape the sport as we know it today. The teams and players of the 1970s left an indelible mark on the NFL, and their legacy continues to influence the game more than 50 years later.

1971

The year 1971 was a significant one for the NFL, as it marked the second year following the merger with the American Football League (AFL). Let's explore the events and developments that took place during this pivotal year in the history of professional football in the United States.

Expansion

In 1971, the NFL added two new teams, the Dallas Cowboys and the Minnesota Vikings. The Cowboys were one of the most successful teams of the 1970s, winning two Super Bowls and becoming one of the most popular franchises in the league. The Vikings also had a successful decade, making it to four Super Bowls but unfortunately losing each time.

The addition of these teams brought the total number of NFL franchises to 26, divided equally between the NFC and the AFC. The expansion also allowed for a new playoff format, with four division winners and two wild card teams advancing to the playoffs.

Players and Teams

In 1971, the NFL saw the emergence of several players who would go on to become legends of the game. One such player was Pittsburgh Steelers' quarterback Terry Bradshaw, who led his team to their first playoff appearance in over a decade. Bradshaw was known for his strong arm and clutch performances in big games, and would go on to lead the Steelers to four Super Bowl victories in the 1970s.

Another notable player from the 1971 season was Miami Dolphins' running back Larry Csonka. Csonka was a key player on the Dolphins' championship teams of the early 1970s, known for his powerful running style and ability to break tackles.

In addition to individual players, several teams stood out during the 1971 season. The Dallas Cowboys, led by quarterback Roger Staubach and running back Duane Thomas, had one of the best offenses in the league, finishing the regular season with a record of 11-3. The Baltimore Colts, led by quarterback Johnny Unitas, also had a strong season, finishing with a record of 10-4 and making it to the playoffs.

Super Bowl VI

Super Bowl VI was played on January 16, 1972, at Tulane Stadium in New Orleans, Louisiana. The game featured the Dallas Cowboys, who were making their second Super Bowl appearance, and the Miami Dolphins, who were playing in their first Super Bowl.

The Cowboys were led by quarterback Roger Staubach, who had taken over the starting role late in the season and helped the team win the NFC championship. The Dolphins were led by quarterback Bob Griese and a strong defense that had allowed the fewest points in the AFC that season.

The game started with a slow pace, with both teams struggling to score in the first quarter. However, the Cowboys broke the deadlock in the second quarter with a 29-yard field goal by Mike Clark. The Dolphins responded with a field goal of their own, but the Cowboys scored two more touchdowns before halftime, a one-yard run by Duane Thomas and a 7-yard pass from Staubach to Lance Alworth.

In the second half, the Cowboys continued to dominate the game, with Staubach completing 12 of 19 passes for 119 yards and two touchdowns. The Dolphins managed to score one touchdown in the fourth quarter, but it was not enough, and the Cowboys won the game 24-3.

Roger Staubach was named the game's Most Valuable Player (MVP) for his outstanding performance, completing 12 of 19 passes for 119 yards and two touchdowns. The Cowboys' defense was also impressive, intercepting two of Griese's passes and holding the Dolphins to only three points.

Super Bowl VI was a significant moment in the history of the Dallas Cowboys, as it was their first Super Bowl victory and solidified their reputation as one of the best teams in the NFL. The game also marked the end of the Miami Dolphins' remarkable undefeated season, as they suffered their first and only loss of the year.

Super Bowl VI was a dominant performance by the Dallas Cowboys, who secured their first-ever Super Bowl victory and established themselves as one of the best teams in the NFL. Roger Staubach's outstanding performance earned him the game's Most Valuable Player award, while the Cowboys' defense played a key role in limiting the Dolphins to only three points.

The year 1971 was a pivotal one for the National Football League, as the league continued to expand and develop following the merger with the American Football League. The addition of new teams and players helped to fuel the growth of the sport, and the emergence of legendary players such as Terry Bradshaw and Larry Csonka helped to establish the NFL as one of the most popular professional sports leagues in the world. The 1971 season was also notable for the Dallas Cowboys' first Super Bowl victory, a sign of the success that was to come for the team in the following years.

1972: A perfect season

The year 1972 was a historic year for the NFL. It was a season marked by records, legends, and epic performances that would forever change the sport. In this section, we will explore the significant events and developments that took place during this season, which would later be known as one of the most iconic seasons in NFL history.

Miami Dolphins' Perfect Season

The highlight of the 1972 NFL season was undoubtedly the Miami Dolphins' perfect season. Under the leadership of head coach Don Shula, the Dolphins went undefeated in the regular season, finishing with a record of 14-0.

Records and Milestones

The 1972 season was also notable for several individual records and milestones. One of the most significant was Franco Harris' "Immaculate Reception" in a playoff game between the Pittsburgh Steelers and the Oakland Raiders. In the closing seconds of the game, Harris caught a deflected pass and ran it in for the game-winning touchdown, a play that has gone down in NFL folklore.

In addition to the "Immaculate Reception," several other records were broken during the 1972 season. Dallas Cowboys' running back Duane Thomas became the first player in NFL history to rush for 1,000 yards in each of his first two seasons, while San Diego Chargers' quarterback Dan Fouts threw for a then-record 4,082 yards.

Expansion

The 1972 season also saw the addition of two new teams to the NFL, the Seattle Seahawks and the Tampa Bay Buccaneers. The expansion brought the total number of teams in the league to 26, with the Seahawks joining the AFC and the Buccaneers joining the NFC.

Notable Players and Teams

Several players and teams stood out during the 1972 season. In addition to the Miami Dolphins' perfect season, the Pittsburgh Steelers had a dominant season, finishing with a record of 11-3 and reaching the playoffs for the first time in eight years. The Steelers were led by a strong defense, which included future Hall of Famers "Mean" Joe Greene and Jack Ham.

On the offensive side of the ball, several players had standout seasons. Running backs Larry Csonka of the Miami Dolphins and O.J. Simpson of the Buffalo Bills both rushed for over 1,200 yards, while Dallas Cowboys' quarterback Roger Staubach led his team to a 10-4 record and a playoff appearance.

Super Bowl VII

Super Bowl VII was played on January 14, 1973, at the Los Angeles Memorial Coliseum in Los Angeles, California. The game featured the Miami Dolphins, who were making their second Super Bowl appearance, and the Washington Redskins, who were playing in their first Super Bowl.

The Dolphins were coming off an undefeated regular season, and were considered heavy favorites going into the game. The Redskins, however, were not intimidated and played a strong defensive game, holding the Dolphins to only two field goals in the first half.

In the second half, the Dolphins' offense came to life, with running back Larry Csonka rushing for 112 yards and a touchdown. The Dolphins also scored a touchdown on a 28-yard interception return by safety Jake Scott, who was named the game's Most Valuable Player (MVP) for his outstanding performance.

The Redskins managed to score a touchdown in the fourth quarter, but it was not enough, and the Dolphins held on to win the game 14-7. The victory secured the Dolphins' perfect season, with a record of 17-0, a feat that has yet to be matched by any team in NFL history.

Super Bowl VII was a significant moment in NFL history, as the Miami Dolphins became the first and only team to complete a perfect season, winning all of their regular season games, playoff games, and the Super Bowl. The game also marked the end of the Washington Redskins' remarkable run to the Super Bowl, as they had won five consecutive games to reach the championship game.

Super Bowl VII was a historic moment in NFL history, as the Miami Dolphins completed a perfect season and secured their second Super Bowl victory. The game was closely contested, with the Dolphins' defense and special teams playing a key role in securing the victory. Jake Scott's outstanding performance earned him the game's Most Valuable Player award, while Larry Csonka's dominant rushing performance was also a highlight of the game.

The 1972 NFL season was a historic one, marked by the Miami Dolphins' perfect season, several individual records and milestones, and the addition of two new teams to the league. The season also saw the emergence of several legendary players and teams that would continue to dominate the league for years to come. The Dolphins' perfect season, in particular, would go down in NFL history as one of the greatest achievements in the sport.

1973

The year 1973 was a season of change and transformation for the NFL. With the addition of new teams and the rise of young players, the league was in a state of transition. In this section, we will explore the significant events and developments that took place during this season, which would later be known as a turning point in the NFL's history.

Expansion

The NFL expanded once again in 1973, adding two new teams to the league. The New Orleans Saints joined the NFC, while the Houston Oilers joined the AFC. The addition of these teams brought the total number of NFL teams to 28, a sign of the league's growing popularity and success.

The Miami Dolphins' Dynasty

The Miami Dolphins continued their dominance in the 1973 season, following their perfect season in 1972. Led by head coach Don Shula and quarterback Bob Griese, the Dolphins finished the season with a record of 12-2, winning their second consecutive AFC East division title.

In the playoffs, the Dolphins faced the Oakland Raiders in the AFC Championship game. In a hard-fought battle, the Dolphins emerged victorious, winning the game 27-10. They then faced the Minnesota Vikings in Super Bowl VIII.

Super Bowl VIII

Super Bowl VIII was played on January 13, 1974, at Rice Stadium in Houston, Texas. The game featured the Miami Dolphins, who were representing the American Football Conference (AFC), and the Minnesota Vikings, who were representing the National Football Conference (NFC).

The Miami Dolphins were coached by Don Shula, and they came into the game with an impressive 15-2 record, having won the AFC Championship game against the Oakland Raiders. The Minnesota Vikings, on the other hand, were coached by Bud Grant and had a record of 12-3-1. They had defeated the Dallas Cowboys in the NFC Championship game to reach the Super Bowl.

The game started with a bang as the Dolphins' special teams unit scored a touchdown on the opening kickoff. Miami's kicker, Garo Yepremian, booted the ball deep into the Vikings' end zone, and Minnesota returner Bill Brown was tackled at the 6-yard line. On the very next play, Vikings quarterback Fran Tarkenton dropped back to pass, but was sacked in the end zone by Dolphins defensive lineman Manny Fernandez for a safety.

After the safety, the Dolphins got the ball back and drove down the field for a touchdown. Running back Larry Csonka scored on a 5-yard run to give Miami a 9-0 lead. The Vikings responded with a long drive of their own, but they were forced to settle for a field goal, cutting the Dolphins' lead to 9-3.

In the second quarter, the Dolphins extended their lead with another touchdown. Quarterback Bob Griese connected with tight end Jim Mandich on a 7-yard pass to make it 16-3. The Vikings tried to mount a comeback, but they were unable to score any more points in the first half.

In the second half, the Dolphins' defense continued to dominate. They intercepted Tarkenton three times and held the Vikings to just 119 yards rushing. Meanwhile, Miami's offense kept the pressure on, with Csonka scoring another touchdown on a 2-yard run in the third quarter. The Dolphins would add one more touchdown in the fourth quarter, with fullback Jim Kiick scoring from 1 yard out to make it 24-7.

The game ended with the Dolphins winning their second consecutive Super Bowl, and completing a perfect season with a 17-0 record. Csonka was named the game's Most Valuable Player, rushing for 145 yards and two touchdowns. The Dolphins' defense, meanwhile, held the Vikings to just 133 yards passing and forced four turnovers.

Super Bowl VIII was a dominant performance by the Miami Dolphins, who cemented their place in NFL history with their second straight championship.

The Rise of Young Stars

The 1973 season also saw the emergence of several young players who would go on to become legends in the NFL. One of these players was running back O.J. Simpson of the Buffalo Bills. Simpson rushed for over 2,000 yards, becoming the first player in NFL history to achieve this feat. His incredible performance earned him the NFL's Most Valuable Player award and cemented his place as one of the greatest players of all time.

Another young star who emerged in the 1973 season was Pittsburgh Steelers' quarterback Terry Bradshaw. In just his fourth year in the league, Bradshaw led the Steelers to their first playoff appearance since 1947. Although they lost in the divisional round, Bradshaw's performance showed that he was a talented and promising player.

Notable Teams and Players

Several other teams and players had notable performances during the 1973 season. The Los Angeles Rams, led by quarterback John Hadl, won their division and reached the playoffs for the first time since 1955. The Dallas Cowboys, led by quarterback Roger Staubach, also had a strong season, finishing with a record of 10-4 and reaching the playoffs.

On the defensive side of the ball, Minnesota Vikings' defensive tackle Alan Page had a standout season, earning the NFL's Defensive Player of the Year award. Page's dominance helped the Vikings win their division and reach the playoffs, where they lost to the Dallas Cowboys in the divisional round.

The 1973 NFL season was a significant year for the league, marked by expansion, the rise of young stars, and the continuation of the Miami Dolphins' dynasty. The addition of new teams showed the growing popularity and success of the NFL, while the emergence of young players signaled a changing of the guard in the league. The 1973 season would set the stage for future seasons, as the NFL continued to evolve and transform.

1974

The NFL of 1974 was a time of significant change and growth for the league. It was a year marked by new rule changes, expansion teams, and memorable games.

Rule Changes

The NFL implemented several rule changes in 1974 aimed at improving player safety and increasing offensive production. One significant change was the introduction of the "five-yard chuck" rule, which prohibited defenders from making contact with a receiver beyond five yards from the line of scrimmage. This rule change opened up passing lanes and led to an increase in passing yards and touchdowns.

Another significant change was the introduction of the "in the grasp" rule, which protected quarterbacks from unnecessary hits by allowing officials to whistle a play dead if the quarterback was deemed "in the grasp" of a defender. This rule change was a precursor to modern-day roughing the passer penalties and helped to increase quarterback safety.

Expansion Teams

The NFL added two new teams in 1974: the Tampa Bay Buccaneers and the Seattle Seahawks. Both teams struggled in their inaugural seasons, with the Buccaneers going 0-14 and the Seahawks finishing with a record of 2-12. Despite their struggles, the addition of these two teams helped to expand the league's reach and popularity.

Memorable Games

Several memorable games took place in the 1974 NFL season, including Super Bowl IX between the Pittsburgh Steelers and the Minnesota Vikings.

Super Bowl IX

Super Bowl IX was played on January 12, 1975, at Tulane Stadium in New Orleans, Louisiana. The game featured the Pittsburgh Steelers, who were representing the American Football Conference (AFC), and the Minnesota Vikings, who were representing the National Football Conference (NFC).

The Pittsburgh Steelers were coached by Chuck Noll and came into the game with a 10-3-1 record, having won the AFC Championship game against the Oakland Raiders. The Minnesota Vikings, coached by Bud Grant, had a record of 12-2 and had defeated the Los Angeles Rams in the NFC Championship game to reach the Super Bowl.

The game started off slowly, with both teams struggling to move the ball on offense. The first quarter was scoreless, but the Steelers' defense made a big play early on when defensive tackle Joe Greene forced a fumble by Vikings running back Dave Osborn, which was recovered by the Steelers.

In the second quarter, the Steelers finally got on the scoreboard. Kicker Roy Gerela connected on a 30-yard field goal to give Pittsburgh a 3-0 lead. The Vikings responded with a long drive, but they were stopped just short of the goal line, and had to settle for a field goal by kicker Fred Cox to tie the game at 3-3.

The third quarter was another defensive battle, with neither team able to score. However, the Steelers' defense made another big play when linebacker Jack Ham intercepted a pass from Vikings quarterback Fran Tarkenton and returned it 10 yards to set up the go-ahead score.

In the fourth quarter, the Steelers' offense finally got into gear. Quarterback Terry Bradshaw led a long drive that was capped off by a 4-yard touchdown run by running back Franco Harris, giving Pittsburgh a 10-3 lead. Later in the quarter, the Steelers' defense made another big play when linebacker Dwight White sacked Tarkenton in the end zone for a safety, making it 12-3.

The Vikings made one last push in the closing minutes, driving deep into Pittsburgh territory. However, the Steelers' defense held strong, and the game ended with Pittsburgh winning their first Super Bowl title by a score of 16-6.

Harris was named the game's Most Valuable Player, rushing for 158 yards and a touchdown on 34 carries. The Steelers' defense was also dominant, holding the Vikings to just 119 yards passing and intercepting Tarkenton three times.

Super Bowl IX was a hard-fought defensive battle, but the Pittsburgh Steelers came out on top, earning their first Super Bowl championship in franchise history. The game marked the beginning of a dynasty for the Steelers, who would go on to win four Super Bowls in six years.

Another memorable game was the "Immaculate Reception" game between the Steelers and the Oakland Raiders. The game was played on December 23, 1972, at Three Rivers Stadium in Pittsburgh, Pennsylvania. With the Steelers trailing 7-6 and just seconds remaining in the game, quarterback Terry Bradshaw threw a pass to running back Franco Harris, who caught the ball after it deflected off of Raiders' safety Jack Tatum. Harris then ran the ball in for a touchdown, giving the Steelers a dramatic 13-7 victory.

The NFL in 1974 was a time of change and growth for the league. The implementation of new rule changes helped to improve player safety and increase offensive production. The addition of two new teams helped to expand the league's reach and popularity, and several memorable games were played, including Super Bowl IX and the "Immaculate Reception" game. Overall, the 1974 NFL season was an important chapter in the league's history, paving the way for future growth and success.

1975

The year 1975 was an exciting time for the NFL. The league was expanding, new stars were emerging, and rivalries were heating up.

Expansion

The NFL added another two expansion teams in 1975: the Seattle Seahawks and the Tampa Bay Buccaneers. Both teams struggled in their second year, with the Buccaneers going 2-12 and the Seahawks finishing with a record of 2-12-0.

Star Players

The 1975 NFL season saw the emergence of several star players, including quarterbacks Roger Staubach of the Dallas Cowboys and Fran Tarkenton of the Minnesota

Vikings. Staubach led the Cowboys to a 10-4 record and a playoff berth, while Tarkenton threw for over 3,000 yards and led the Vikings to an 11-2-1 record.

Rivalries

One of the most heated rivalries of the 1975 NFL season was between the Dallas Cowboys and the Washington Redskins. The two teams faced off twice during the regular season, with the Cowboys winning both games by a combined score of 41-14. However, the Redskins would have the last laugh, defeating the Cowboys in the playoffs to advance to the Super Bowl.

Another memorable rivalry of the 1975 season was between the Pittsburgh Steelers and the Oakland Raiders. The two teams met in the AFC Championship Game, with the Steelers emerging victorious by a score of 16-10. The game was marked by a controversial call in which the Steelers' Franco Harris caught a deflected pass and ran it in for a touchdown, now known as the "Immaculate Reception."

Super Bowl X

Super Bowl X was played on January 18, 1976, at the Orange Bowl in Miami, Florida. The game featured the Pittsburgh Steelers, who were representing the American Football Conference (AFC), and the Dallas Cowboys, who were representing the National Football Conference (NFC).

The Pittsburgh Steelers were coached by Chuck Noll and came into the game with a 12-2 record, having won the AFC Championship game against the Oakland Raiders. The Dallas Cowboys, coached by Tom Landry, had a record of 10-4 and had defeated the Los Angeles Rams in the NFC Championship game to reach the Super Bowl.

The game started off with a flurry of scoring. The Steelers' special teams unit scored the game's first touchdown when receiver Lynn Swann returned a punt 34 yards for a score. The Cowboys responded with a touchdown of their own, as quarterback Roger Staubach connected with receiver Percy Howard on a 34-yard pass to tie the game at 7-7.

In the second quarter, the Steelers' defense made a big play when defensive back Glen Edwards intercepted a pass from Staubach and returned it to the Dallas 7-yard line. Two plays later, running back Franco Harris scored on a 9-yard run to give Pittsburgh a 14-7 lead.

The Cowboys responded with a field goal by kicker Toni Fritsch to cut the lead to 14-10, but the Steelers extended their lead just before halftime with a field goal by kicker Roy Gerela, making it 17-10.

In the third quarter, the Cowboys tied the game once again when Staubach threw a 7-yard touchdown pass to tight end Jean Fugett. However, the Steelers regained the lead late in the quarter when Bradshaw hit Swann with a 64-yard touchdown pass, making it 24-17.

The fourth quarter was a defensive battle, with neither team able to score until the Cowboys' offense finally got into gear with just over two minutes left in the game. Staubach led a long drive down the field and hit receiver Drew Pearson with a 34-yard touchdown pass to tie the game at 24-24.

However, the Steelers would not be denied. Bradshaw led a quick drive down the field, setting up a game-winning field goal by Gerela from 36 yards out with just seconds left on the clock. The Steelers won the game by a score of 27-24, earning their second Super Bowl championship in franchise history.

Swann was named the game's Most Valuable Player, catching four passes for 161 yards and a touchdown. Harris also had a strong game, rushing for 82 yards and a touchdown on 20 carries. The game is remembered as one of the most exciting Super Bowls of all time, with both teams playing at a high level and the outcome in doubt until the very end.

The 1975 NFL season was an exciting time for the league. Expansion continued, new stars emerged, and heated rivalries developed. The Pittsburgh Steelers cemented their place as one of the dominant teams of the era, winning their second consecutive Super Bowl. Overall, the 1975 NFL season was a memorable chapter in the league's history.

1976

The NFL of 1976 was a season of significant change and upheaval. The league was expanding once again, with the addition of two new teams, and a number of rule changes were implemented to improve player safety and increase offensive production.

Expansion

The NFL added two new teams in 1976: the Seattle Seahawks and the Tampa Bay Buccaneers. The Seahawks improved on their previous season, finishing with a record of 2-12, while the Buccaneers continued to struggle, going winless at 0-14. The addition of these two teams helped to expand the league's reach and popularity.

Rule Changes

The NFL implemented several rule changes in 1976 aimed at improving player safety and increasing offensive production. One significant change was the introduction of the "touchback" rule, which allowed a team to start their next possession on their own 20-yard line if the opposing team kicked the ball into the end zone. This rule change encouraged more touchbacks, reducing the number of high-speed collisions on kickoffs.

Another significant rule change was the introduction of the "blow to the head" penalty, which prohibited any blow to the head or neck area of a defenseless player. This rule change helped to reduce head injuries and concussions, improving player safety.

Star Players

The 1976 NFL season saw the emergence of several star players, including quarterbacks Ken Stabler of the Oakland Raiders and Bert Jones of the Baltimore Colts. Stabler led the Raiders to an 11-3 record and a playoff berth, while Jones threw for over 3,000 yards and led the Colts to a 11-3 record as well.

Rivalries

One of the most heated rivalries of the 1976 NFL season was between the Dallas Cowboys and the Los Angeles Rams. The two teams faced off in the NFC Championship Game, with the Cowboys emerging victorious by a score of 37-7. The Cowboys would go on to lose to the Pittsburgh Steelers in Super Bowl X.

Super Bowl XI

Super Bowl XI was played on January 9, 1977, at the Rose Bowl in Pasadena, California. The game featured the Oakland Raiders, who were representing the American Football Conference (AFC), and the Minnesota Vikings, who were representing the National Football Conference (NFC).

The Oakland Raiders were coached by John Madden and came into the game with a 13-1 record, having won the AFC Championship game against the Pittsburgh Steelers. The Minnesota Vikings, coached by Bud Grant, had a record of 11-2-1 and had defeated the Los Angeles Rams in the NFC Championship game to reach the Super Bowl.

The game started off slowly, with both teams struggling to move the ball on offense. The first quarter was scoreless, but the Raiders' defense made a big play early on when defensive end Willie Jones intercepted a pass from Vikings quarterback Fran Tarkenton and returned it to the Minnesota 31-yard line.

In the second quarter, the Raiders finally got on the scoreboard. Kicker Errol Mann connected on a 24-yard field goal to give Oakland a 3-0 lead. The Vikings responded with a long drive, but they were stopped just short of the goal line, and had to settle for a field goal by kicker Fred Cox to tie the game at 3-3.

The Raiders' offense finally got going late in the second quarter. Quarterback Ken Stabler led a long drive that was capped off by a 1-yard touchdown run by running back Mark van Eeghen, giving Oakland a 10-3 lead at halftime.

In the third quarter, the Raiders' offense continued to dominate. Stabler hit receiver Fred Biletnikoff with a 48-yard touchdown pass to extend Oakland's lead to 17-3. The Vikings finally got on the scoreboard with a touchdown by running back Brent McClanahan, but the Raiders responded with another touchdown run by van Eeghen to make it 24-10.

In the fourth quarter, the Raiders' defense sealed the game with two interceptions of Tarkenton, one by cornerback Skip Thomas and another by linebacker Willie Hall. Oakland won the game by a score of 32-14, earning their first Super Bowl championship in franchise history.

Stabler was named the game's Most Valuable Player, completing 12 of 19 passes for 180 yards and a touchdown. Van Eeghen also had a strong game, rushing for 73 yards and two touchdowns on 18 carries. The Raiders' defense was dominant, holding the Vikings to just 119 yards passing and intercepting Tarkenton three times.

Super Bowl XI was a decisive victory for the Oakland Raiders, who played a strong game on both offense and defense. The game marked the beginning of a successful era for the Raiders, who would go on to win two more Super Bowl championships in the following decade.

The NFL in 1976 was a season marked by expansion, rule changes, and memorable games. The addition of two new teams helped to expand the league's reach and popularity, while new rule changes improved player safety and increased offensive production. The Pittsburgh Steelers continued their dominance, winning their third Super Bowl, while emerging stars like Ken Stabler and Bert Jones solidified their place in NFL history. Overall, the 1976 NFL season was an important chapter in the league's history, paving the way for future growth and success.

1977

The 1977 NFL season was a time of growth and transition for the league. New stars emerged, existing rivalries intensified, and the NFL saw the debut of its first ever wildcard playoff system.

Star Players

The 1977 NFL season saw the emergence of several star players, including running backs Walter Payton of the Chicago Bears and Tony Dorsett of the Dallas Cowboys. Payton rushed for over 1,800 yards and led the Bears to a playoff berth, while Dorsett rushed for over 1,000 yards and helped lead the Cowboys to the Super Bowl.

Rivalries

One of the most intense rivalries of the 1977 NFL season was between the Dallas Cowboys and the Washington Redskins. The two teams faced off twice during the regular season, with the Cowboys winning both games. However, the Redskins would have the last laugh, defeating the Cowboys in the playoffs to advance to the Super Bowl.

Another notable rivalry of the 1977 season was between the Oakland Raiders and the Denver Broncos. The two teams met twice during the regular season, with each team winning one game. They would meet once again in the playoffs, with the Raiders emerging victorious in a close game.

Wildcard Playoff System

The 1977 NFL season marked the debut of the wildcard playoff system. The system allowed for a total of five teams from each conference to qualify for the playoffs, with the three division winners and two wildcard teams. This allowed for more teams to have a chance at the postseason, and added an extra layer of excitement to the end of the regular season.

Super Bowl XII

Super Bowl XII was the championship game of the 1977 NFL season, played on January 15, 1978, at the Louisiana Superdome in New Orleans, Louisiana. The game was contested between the Dallas Cowboys and the Denver Broncos, and it was the first Super Bowl played indoors. The game featured two dominant defenses and was a lopsided affair, with the Cowboys winning 27-10.

The Cowboys entered the game as heavy favorites, having finished the regular season with a 12-2 record and dominating their opponents in the playoffs. The Broncos, on the other hand, had squeaked into the playoffs with a 12-2 record and had pulled off two upsets to make it to the Super Bowl.

The game started out with a bang for the Cowboys, as they scored on their second possession of the game with a 29-yard touchdown pass from quarterback Roger Staubach to wide receiver Butch Johnson. The Broncos responded with a 45-yard field goal from kicker Jim Turner to cut the lead to 7-3. However, the Cowboys quickly regained control of the game, scoring two more touchdowns in the second quarter to take a commanding 20-3 lead at halftime.

The Cowboys defense was the star of the game, forcing eight turnovers and sacking Broncos quarterback Craig Morton four times. They held the Broncos to just 156 yards of total offense, including only 61 passing yards. The Broncos' lone touchdown came on a fumble recovery in the end zone in the third quarter.

The Cowboys offense, led by Staubach and running back Tony Dorsett, was also impressive, racking up 345 yards of total offense. Dorsett finished the game with 96 rushing yards and a touchdown, while Staubach threw for 183 yards and one touchdown.

The game was not without controversy, as the Cowboys' "Doomsday Defense" was accused of playing dirty and intentionally injuring Broncos players. Broncos tight end Riley Odoms suffered a concussion and had to leave the game, while running back Rob Lytle injured his shoulder.

Despite the controversy, the Cowboys' dominant performance secured their second Super Bowl victory in five years, and they were hailed as one of the greatest teams in NFL history. Staubach was named the game's Most Valuable Player, and the Cowboys' defense was lauded for its suffocating performance.

Super Bowl XII was a memorable game for Cowboys fans and a disappointing one for Broncos fans. It marked the beginning of a new era in the NFL, as the league started to shift towards a more pass-oriented game, and it set the stage for some of the most iconic moments in Super Bowl history.

The 1977 NFL season was a time of growth and transition for the league. The emergence of new stars like Walter Payton and Tony Dorsett, along with the intensification of existing rivalries, added excitement and intrigue to the season. The introduction of the wildcard playoff system allowed for more teams to have a chance at the postseason, while the Dallas Cowboys cemented their place as one of the dominant teams of the era, winning their second Super Bowl. Overall, the 1977 NFL season was an important chapter in the league's history, paving the way for future growth and success.

1978

The NFL in the year 1978 was an exciting time for the league, with some of the biggest stars in the history of the game taking the field.

Key Events

One of the biggest events of the 1978 NFL season was the decision to expand the playoffs from eight teams to ten. This allowed more teams to make the postseason and gave fans more exciting matchups to watch. In addition to the playoff expansion, the NFL also introduced a new rule that allowed offensive linemen to extend their arms and use their hands when blocking.

Another key event that took place in 1978 was the retirement of legendary quarterback Johnny Unitas. Unitas had played for 18 seasons in the NFL, winning three championships and setting numerous records along the way. His retirement marked the end of an era in the league.

Players

The 1978 NFL season featured some of the greatest players in the history of the game. One of the most notable players from this season was running back Earl Campbell, who was drafted by the Houston Oilers with the first overall pick in the 1978 NFL Draft. Campbell would go on to win the Rookie of the Year award and lead the league in rushing with 1,450 yards.

Another standout player from the 1978 season was Walter Payton, the running back for the Chicago Bears. Payton led the league in rushing in 1978 with 1,395 yards and also set a record for most rushing attempts in a season with 333. Payton's performance helped the Bears reach the playoffs for the first time since 1963.

Storylines

One of the biggest storylines of the 1978 season was the battle for the AFC East division title between the Miami

Dolphins and the New England Patriots. The two teams were tied with identical 10-4 records going into their final game of the season, which was played in Foxboro, Massachusetts. The Patriots won the game 33-14, clinching the division title and earning a spot in the playoffs.

Super Bowl XIII

Another storyline from the 1978 season was the dominance of the Pittsburgh Steelers, who won their third Super Bowl championship in five years.

Super Bowl XIII was the championship game of the 1978 NFL season, played on January 21, 1979, at the Orange Bowl in Miami, Florida. The game featured a rematch of Super Bowl X between the Pittsburgh Steelers and the Dallas Cowboys, and it was a thrilling shootout that ended with the Steelers winning their third Super Bowl in five years, 35-31.

The game started off with a bang, as Steelers quarterback Terry Bradshaw threw a 28-yard touchdown pass to wide receiver John Stallworth on the team's second possession. The Cowboys responded with a 7-yard touchdown pass from quarterback Roger Staubach to tight end Jackie Smith to tie the game at 7-7.

The Steelers took control of the game in the second quarter, scoring three touchdowns to take a 21-point lead. The first was a 75-yard touchdown pass from Bradshaw to Stallworth, followed by a 1-yard touchdown run by running back Franco Harris, and then another 7-yard touchdown pass from Bradshaw to Stallworth.

The Cowboys mounted a comeback in the second half, with Staubach throwing two touchdown passes to wide receiver Butch Johnson and another to tight end Billy Joe DuPree.

However, the Steelers managed to hold on to their lead, thanks in part to a crucial interception by safety Mike Wagner in the fourth quarter.

Bradshaw had a stellar game, throwing for 318 yards and four touchdowns, and he was named the game's Most Valuable Player. Stallworth was also outstanding, with three touchdown receptions and 115 receiving yards.

The game was notable for its high-scoring, back-and-forth nature, as well as for its impact on the future of the NFL. The game was watched by over 79 million people, making it the most-watched program in television history at the time. It also marked the beginning of a new era of passing offenses in the NFL, as both teams threw the ball more than they ran it and combined for over 800 yards of total offense.

Super Bowl XIII was a thrilling game that showcased some of the best talent in NFL history, and it remains one of the most memorable Super Bowls of all time. The Steelers' victory cemented their place as one of the greatest dynasties in NFL history, and it set the stage for even more exciting and high-scoring Super Bowls in the years to come.

The 1978 NFL season was an exciting time for the league, with many of the game's biggest stars taking the field. The decision to expand the playoffs and introduce new rules helped to make the game even more exciting for fans, while the retirement of Johnny Unitas marked the end of an era in the league. Overall, the 1978 season was a memorable one for fans of the NFL.

1979

The year 1979 marked the end of the decade and the beginning of a new era for the NFL.

Key Events

One of the most significant events of the 1979 NFL season was the implementation of a new rule regarding sudden-death overtime. The rule change meant that if a game ended in a tie at the end of regulation, the teams would continue playing until one team scored a point. This change made the game more exciting and led to some unforgettable moments.

Another significant event that took place in 1979 was the inauguration of the Hall of Fame Game, which was played between the New York Jets and the Washington Redskins. This game was the first-ever played in the newly built Pro Football Hall of Fame Stadium in Canton, Ohio.

Players

The 1979 NFL season featured some of the greatest players in the history of the game. One of the most notable players from this season was running back O.J. Simpson, who was playing for the San Francisco 49ers. Simpson rushed for 1,053 yards and scored four touchdowns during the 1979 season.

Another standout player from the 1979 season was quarterback Dan Fouts of the San Diego Chargers. Fouts set a new NFL record for most passing yards in a single season, throwing for 4,082 yards and 24 touchdowns. He also led the league in completions, attempts, and yards per game.

Storylines

One of the most significant storylines from the 1979 season was the success of the Pittsburgh Steelers. The Steelers won their fourth Super Bowl championship in six years, defeating the Los Angeles Rams 31-19 in Super Bowl XIV. The game was played at the Rose Bowl in Pasadena, California, and was watched by a record-breaking television audience of over 76 million viewers.

Another significant storyline from the 1979 season was the rise of the Dallas Cowboys. The team had missed the playoffs for the past two seasons, but in 1979 they finished with an 11-5 record and reached the playoffs as a wild card team. They won their first playoff game against the Atlanta Falcons but lost in the divisional round to the Rams.

Super Bowl XIV

Super Bowl XIV was the championship game of the 1979 NFL season, played on January 20, 1980, at the Rose Bowl in Pasadena, California. The game featured the Pittsburgh Steelers, who were looking to win their fourth Super Bowl in six years, and the Los Angeles Rams, who were making their first Super Bowl appearance in franchise history.

The game was a closely contested affair, with both teams trading blows throughout. The Steelers struck first with a 31-yard touchdown pass from quarterback Terry Bradshaw to wide receiver John Stallworth, but the Rams responded with a 50-yard touchdown pass from quarterback Vince Ferragamo to wide receiver Ron Smith to tie the game at 7-7.

The Steelers took the lead again in the second quarter, with a 7-yard touchdown run by running back Franco Harris, but the Rams answered with a 24-yard field goal from kicker Frank Corral to cut the lead to 14-10 at halftime.

The Rams took their first lead of the game in the third quarter, with a 1-yard touchdown run by fullback Cullen Bryant, but the Steelers quickly regained the lead with a 73-yard touchdown pass from Bradshaw to Stallworth. The Rams tied the game again with a 24-yard field goal by Corral in the fourth quarter.

With less than two minutes remaining in the game, the Steelers mounted a game-winning drive, highlighted by a 45-yard reception by Stallworth. The drive culminated in a 1-yard touchdown run by running back Rocky Bleier, giving the Steelers a 31-19 lead with just seconds left on the clock. The Rams managed to score a late touchdown, but it was too little, too late, and the Steelers held on for a 31-28 victory.

Bradshaw had another outstanding game, throwing for 309 yards and two touchdowns, while Stallworth was named the game's Most Valuable Player with 121 receiving yards and a touchdown.

Super Bowl XIV was a fitting end to the Steelers' dynasty of the 1970s, as they won their fourth Super Bowl in six years and solidified their place as one of the greatest teams in NFL history. The game also showcased the talents of some of the best players of the era, including Bradshaw, Stallworth, Harris, and Ferragamo.

Overall, Super Bowl XIV was a thrilling and closely contested game that provided fans with plenty of excitement and drama. It was a fitting end to one of the greatest eras in NFL history, and it set the stage for even more memorable Super Bowls in the years to come.

The 1979 NFL season was a memorable one, with many significant events, players, and storylines. The implementation of sudden-death overtime added a new level of excitement to the game, while the inauguration of the Hall of Fame Game was a historic moment for the league. The dominance of the Pittsburgh Steelers continued, and the rise of the Dallas Cowboys gave fans something new to cheer for. Overall, the 1979 season was a fitting end to a decade that had seen the NFL grow into the juggernaut it is today.

THE 1980'S

1980

The year 1980 marked the beginning of a new decade for the NFL. The league had continued to grow in popularity throughout the 1970s, and the 1980s promised to be just as exciting.

Key Events

One of the most significant events of the 1980 NFL season was the expansion of the league. The league added two new teams, the Tampa Bay Buccaneers and the Seattle Seahawks, bringing the total number of teams to 28. This expansion marked the first time the league had grown since 1976.

Another significant event that took place in 1980 was the decision to change the playoff format. The league expanded the playoffs from ten teams to twelve, allowing more teams to make the postseason and giving fans more exciting matchups to watch.

Players

The 1980 NFL season featured some of the greatest players in the history of the game. One of the most notable players from this season was running back Earl Campbell of the Houston Oilers. Campbell rushed for 1,934 yards and scored 13 touchdowns during the 1980 season, earning him the Most Valuable Player award.

Another standout player from the 1980 season was quarterback Brian Sipe of the Cleveland Browns. Sipe threw for 4,132 yards and 30 touchdowns, leading the Browns to the playoffs for the first time in seven years.

Storylines

One of the most significant storylines from the 1980 season was the rise of the San Francisco 49ers. The team had finished with a 6-10 record in 1979 but rebounded in 1980, finishing with a 13-3 record and reaching the playoffs for the first time in eight years. The 49ers were led by quarterback Joe Montana, who threw for 3,565 yards and 19 touchdowns during the season.

Another significant storyline from the 1980 season was the success of the Philadelphia Eagles. The team finished with a 12-4 record, winning their first division title since 1960. The Eagles were led by quarterback Ron Jaworski, who threw for 3,529 yards and 27 touchdowns during the season.

Super Bowl XV

Super Bowl XV was the championship game of the 1980 NFL season, played on January 25, 1981, at the Louisiana Superdome in New Orleans, Louisiana. The game featured the Philadelphia Eagles, who were making their first Super Bowl appearance in franchise history, and the Oakland Raiders, who were looking to win their second Super Bowl in four years.

The game started off slowly, with both teams struggling to move the ball in the first quarter. The Eagles struck first with a 30-yard field goal by kicker Tony Franklin early in the second quarter, but the Raiders quickly responded with a 2-yard touchdown run by running back Kenny King to take a 7-3 lead.

The Eagles regained the lead later in the second quarter with a 7-yard touchdown pass from quarterback Ron Jaworski to wide receiver Rodney Parker, but the Raiders tied the game at halftime with a 46-yard field goal by kicker Chris Bahr.

The third quarter was dominated by the Raiders, who scored two touchdowns to take a commanding 21-10 lead. The first was a 80-yard touchdown pass from quarterback Jim Plunkett to wide receiver Cliff Branch, and the second was a 2-yard touchdown run by King.

The Eagles mounted a comeback in the fourth quarter, with Jaworski throwing a 7-yard touchdown pass to tight end John Spagnola to cut the lead to 21-17. However, the Raiders put the game away with a 2-yard touchdown run by fullback Mark van Eeghen, giving them a 28-17 victory.

Plunkett was named the game's Most Valuable Player, completing 13 of 21 passes for 261 yards and three touchdowns. King was also outstanding, rushing for 75 yards and two touchdowns.

Super Bowl XV was a historic game, as it was the first Super Bowl to be played in a domed stadium and the first to be broadcast in its entirety on network television. It was also notable for the Raiders' improbable run to the championship, as they had started the season as a wild card team and had to win three playoff games on the road to reach the Super Bowl.

Overall, Super Bowl XV was a memorable and exciting game that showcased the talents of some of the best players of the era. It was a fitting end to the 1980 NFL season, and it set the stage for even more thrilling Super Bowls in the years to come.

The 1980 NFL season was an exciting time for the league, with many significant events, players, and storylines. The expansion of the league and the change to the playoff format added a new level of excitement, while the rise of the San Francisco 49ers and Philadelphia Eagles gave fans something new to cheer for. Overall, the 1980 season was a promising start to a decade that would see the NFL continue to grow in popularity and become the most popular sport in the United States.

1981

The year 1981 was an important year for the NFL. It marked the beginning of the 1980s and the continuation of the league's growth in popularity.

Key Events

One of the most significant events of the 1981 NFL season was the NFL Players Association (NFLPA) strike. The strike began on September 20th and lasted for 57 days, causing the cancellation of seven weeks of games. The strike was eventually settled, but it had a significant impact on the league and its fans.

Another significant event that took place in 1981 was the first-ever regular-season game played outside of the United States. The game was played in London, England, between the Chicago Bears and the Dallas Cowboys, with the Bears winning 17-6.

Players

The 1981 NFL season featured some of the greatest players in the history of the game. One of the most notable players from this season was running back Marcus Allen of the Oakland Raiders. Allen rushed for 697 yards and scored 11 touchdowns during his rookie season, earning him the Rookie of the Year award.

Another standout player from the 1981 season was quarterback Joe Montana of the San Francisco 49ers. Montana threw for 3,565 yards and 19 touchdowns, leading the 49ers to a 13-3 record and a playoff berth.

Storylines

One of the most significant storylines from the 1981 season was the continued success of the San Francisco 49ers. The team had finished with a 6-10 record in 1980 but rebounded in 1981, winning their division and reaching the NFC Championship game. The 49ers were led by Montana and a strong defense, which allowed only 15.6 points per game.

Another significant storyline from the 1981 season was the rise of the Cincinnati Bengals. The team had finished with a 6-10 record in 1980 but improved to a 12-4 record in 1981, winning their division and reaching the playoffs for the first time since 1975. The Bengals were led by quarterback Ken Anderson, who threw for 3,754 yards and 29 touchdowns during the season.

Super Bowl XVI

Super Bowl XVI was the championship game of the 1981 NFL season, played on January 24, 1982, at the Pontiac Silverdome in Pontiac, Michigan. The game featured the San Francisco 49ers, who were making their first Super Bowl appearance in franchise history, and the Cincinnati Bengals, who were also making their first Super Bowl appearance.

The 49ers got off to a quick start, with a 20-yard field goal by kicker Ray Wersching on their first drive of the game. The Bengals responded with a 33-yard field goal by kicker Jim Breech to tie the game at 3-3.

In the second quarter, the 49ers took control of the game with a pair of touchdowns. The first was a 1-yard touchdown run by running back Earl Cooper, and the second was a 11-yard touchdown pass from quarterback Joe Montana to wide receiver Freddie Solomon. The Bengals managed to score a touchdown of their own with a 5-yard run by running back Pete Johnson, but the 49ers went into halftime with a 20-7 lead.

The Bengals mounted a comeback in the second half, with another touchdown run by Johnson and a 4-yard touchdown pass from quarterback Ken Anderson to tight end Dan Ross. However, the 49ers held on for a 26-21 victory, thanks in part to a strong defensive effort that included a key interception by safety Dwight Hicks in the fourth quarter.

Montana was named the game's Most Valuable Player, completing 14 of 22 passes for 157 yards and a touchdown. Cooper was also outstanding, rushing for 58 yards and a touchdown and catching two passes for 18 yards.

Super Bowl XVI was a historic game for the 49ers, as it was their first Super Bowl victory and the first championship in franchise history. It was also notable for the emergence of Montana, who would go on to become one of the greatest quarterbacks in NFL history. The game was also a memorable moment for the city of San Francisco, which had suffered through several losing seasons before the 49ers' rise to the top of the league.

Overall, Super Bowl XVI was an exciting and closely contested game that provided fans with plenty of thrills and drama. It was a fitting end to the 1981 NFL season, and it set the stage for even more memorable Super Bowls in the years to come.

The 1981 NFL season was an exciting time for the league, with many significant events, players, and storylines. The NFLPA strike had a significant impact on the league, while the first regular-season game played outside of the United States opened up new opportunities for the league. The continued success of the San Francisco 49ers and the rise of the Cincinnati Bengals gave fans something new to cheer for. Overall, the 1981 season was a promising continuation of the NFL's growth in popularity and success.

1982

The year 1982 was a challenging year for the NFL. The league faced a players' strike that shortened the regular season and caused a lot of uncertainty among fans.

Key Events

The most significant event of the 1982 NFL season was the players' strike that began on September 20th and lasted for 57 days. The strike caused the cancellation of seven weeks of the regular season, resulting in a shortened season that consisted of only nine games. The strike was eventually settled, and the regular season resumed on November 21st, with the playoffs starting on December 26th.

Another significant event that took place during the 1982 season was the first-ever NFL game played on artificial turf. The game was played between the Pittsburgh Steelers and the Houston Oilers at the Astrodome in Houston, Texas.

Players

The 1982 NFL season featured some of the greatest players in the history of the game. One of the most notable players from this season was running back John Riggins of the

Washington Redskins. Riggins rushed for 1,347 yards and scored a league-high 24 touchdowns during the season, leading the Redskins to a Super Bowl victory over the Miami Dolphins.

Another standout player from the 1982 season was quarterback Dan Fouts of the San Diego Chargers. Fouts threw for 2,883 yards and 17 touchdowns during the season, leading the Chargers to a 6-3 record and a playoff berth.

Storylines

One of the most significant storylines from the 1982 season was the impact of the players' strike on the league. The strike caused a lot of uncertainty among fans and led to a shortened regular season. However, despite the challenges, the NFL was able to resume play and crown a champion in the Washington Redskins.

Another significant storyline from the 1982 season was the success of the Los Angeles Raiders. The Raiders finished the season with an 8-1 record and won their division, eventually reaching the AFC Championship game. The Raiders were led by quarterback Jim Plunkett, who threw for 2,935 yards and 18 touchdowns during the season.

Super Bowl XVII

Super Bowl XVII was the championship game of the 1982 NFL season, played on January 30, 1983, at the Rose Bowl in Pasadena, California. The game featured the Miami Dolphins, who were making their third Super Bowl appearance in franchise history, and the Washington Redskins, who were making their second Super Bowl appearance.

The game was a hard-fought battle, with both teams trading blows throughout the first half. The Dolphins struck first with a 37-yard field goal by kicker Uwe von Schamann, but the Redskins responded with a 70-yard touchdown pass from quarterback Joe Theismann to wide receiver Alvin Garrett. The Dolphins tied the game at 10-10 just before halftime with a 76-yard touchdown run by running back Fulton Walker, but the Redskins took the lead again with a 14-yard touchdown run by running back John Riggins in the third quarter.

The Dolphins mounted a comeback in the fourth quarter, with quarterback David Woodley throwing a 98-yard touchdown pass to wide receiver Jimmy Cefalo to tie the game at 17-17. However, the Redskins responded with a 43-yard field goal by kicker Mark Moseley to take a 20-17 lead.

The game came down to the wire, with the Dolphins driving deep into Redskins territory in the final minutes of the game. On fourth down and 4 yards to go, von Schamann kicked a game-tying field goal from 25 yards out with just 1:56 left on the clock.

The Redskins responded with a clutch drive of their own, with Riggins leading the way with several key runs. With just 10 seconds left in the game, Riggins scored the game-winning touchdown on a 43-yard run, giving the Redskins a 27-17 victory and their first Super Bowl championship in franchise history.

Riggins was named the game's Most Valuable Player, rushing for 166 yards and a touchdown on 38 carries. Theismann was also outstanding, completing 15 of 23 passes for 143 yards and a touchdown.

Super Bowl XVII was a historic game for the Redskins, as they became the first team to win the Super Bowl after losing their first game of the season. It was also a memorable moment for Riggins, who cemented his status as one of the greatest running backs in NFL history with his clutch performance in the game.

Overall, Super Bowl XVII was a thrilling and dramatic game that provided fans with plenty of excitement and entertainment. It was a fitting end to the 1982 NFL season, and it set the stage for even more unforgettable Super Bowls in the years to come.

The 1982 NFL season was a challenging year for the league, with the players' strike causing a lot of uncertainty and a shortened regular season. However, the league was able to overcome these challenges and crown a champion in the Washington Redskins. The success of the Los Angeles Raiders and standout players like John Riggins and Dan Fouts gave fans something to cheer for during a difficult season. Overall, the 1982 season was a reminder of the resilience of the NFL and its ability to overcome adversity.

1983

The 1983 NFL season was a year of change and transition for the league. The season saw the emergence of several young stars and the decline of some of the league's most iconic players.

Key Events

One of the most significant events of the 1983 NFL season was the introduction of instant replay. The NFL adopted instant replay to review questionable calls made by officials on the field. The new system was first used in a game between the Chicago Bears and Tampa Bay Buccaneers on September 25th.

Another important event of the 1983 season was the retirement of legendary Dallas Cowboys quarterback Roger Staubach. Staubach had played for the Cowboys for 11 seasons and won two Super Bowl titles during his career.

Players

The 1983 NFL season featured several young stars who would go on to have Hall of Fame careers. One of the most notable players from this season was San Francisco 49ers quarterback Joe Montana. Montana threw for 3,910 yards and 26 touchdowns during the season, leading the 49ers to a 10-6 record and a playoff berth.

Another standout player from the 1983 season was running back Eric Dickerson of the Los Angeles Rams. Dickerson rushed for 1,808 yards and scored 18 touchdowns during the season, setting an NFL rookie record.

Storylines

One of the most significant storylines from the 1983 season was the emergence of the Washington Redskins as a dominant team in the league. The Redskins finished the season with a 14-2 record and won their division, eventually reaching the Super Bowl. The Redskins were led by quarterback Joe Theismann, who threw for 3,714 yards and 29 touchdowns during the season.

Another significant storyline from the 1983 season was the decline of some of the league's most iconic players. Players like Roger Staubach, Terry Bradshaw, and Franco Harris all retired from the NFL during the season, marking the end of an era for the league.

Super Bowl XVIII

Super Bowl XVIII was the championship game of the 1983 NFL season, played on January 22, 1984, at Tampa Stadium in Tampa, Florida. The game featured the Los Angeles Raiders, who were making their third Super Bowl appearance in franchise history, and the Washington Redskins, who were making their third Super Bowl appearance.

The game was a one-sided affair, with the Raiders dominating from start to finish. The Raiders got off to a quick start with a 12-yard touchdown run by running back Marcus Allen in the first quarter. They extended their lead to 21-3 by halftime, with touchdown passes from quarterback Jim Plunkett to wide receivers Cliff Branch and Malcolm Barnwell.

In the second half, the Raiders continued to dominate, with Allen scoring two more touchdowns on a 5-yard run and a 74-yard run. The Redskins managed to score a touchdown of their own in the fourth quarter on a 6-yard pass from quarterback Joe Theismann to wide receiver Charlie Brown, but it was too little too late. The Raiders went on to win the game 38-9, with Allen being named the game's Most Valuable Player after rushing for 191 yards and two touchdowns on 20 carries.

Super Bowl XVIII was a historic game for the Raiders, as they became the first wild card team to win the Super Bowl. It was also a memorable moment for Allen, who set a Super Bowl record with his 74-yard touchdown run and cemented his status as one of the greatest running backs in NFL history. The game was also notable for Plunkett, who became the first quarterback to win two Super Bowls with different teams.

Overall, Super Bowl XVIII was a dominant performance by the Raiders, who proved themselves to be one of the best teams in the NFL that year. It was a fitting end to the 1983 NFL season, and it set the stage for even more memorable Super Bowls in the years to come.

The 1983 NFL season was a year of change and transition for the league. The introduction of instant replay and the emergence of young stars like Joe Montana and Eric Dickerson signaled a new era for the NFL. The dominance of the Washington Redskins and the retirements of legendary players like Roger Staubach marked the end of an era for the league. Overall, the 1983 season was a reminder that the NFL is constantly evolving and that new stars will always emerge to take the place of the old.

1984

The 1984 NFL season was one of the most exciting and memorable seasons in league history. The season saw the emergence of several young stars, the resurgence of some of the league's most iconic players, and one of the most dominant teams in NFL history.

Key Events

One of the most significant events of the 1984 NFL season was the introduction of the 2-point conversion. The league had previously only allowed for 1-point and 3-point conversions, but the new rule allowed teams to attempt a 2-point conversion after scoring a touchdown. The first 2-point conversion in NFL history was successfully completed by the New York Jets in their season-opening game against the Buffalo Bills.

Another important event of the 1984 season was the retirement of Pittsburgh Steelers quarterback Terry

Bradshaw. Bradshaw had played for the Steelers for 14 seasons and won four Super Bowl titles during his career.

Players

The 1984 NFL season featured some of the league's most iconic and dominant players. One of the most notable players from this season was Miami Dolphins quarterback Dan Marino. Marino threw for 5,084 yards and 48 touchdowns during the season, setting new records for most passing yards and most touchdown passes in a single season. Marino led the Dolphins to a 14-2 record and a Super Bowl appearance.

Another standout player from the 1984 season was San Francisco 49ers wide receiver Jerry Rice. Rice caught 86 passes for 1,570 yards and scored 15 touchdowns during the season, setting new records for most receiving yards and most touchdown receptions in a single season.

Storylines

One of the most significant storylines from the 1984 season was the dominance of the San Francisco 49ers. The 49ers finished the season with a 15-1 record and won their division, eventually winning the Super Bowl. The team was led by quarterback Joe Montana and wide receiver Jerry Rice, who both had historic seasons.

Another significant storyline from the 1984 season was the resurgence of some of the league's most iconic players. Players like Walter Payton of the Chicago Bears, Dan Fouts of the San Diego Chargers, and Marcus Allen of the Los Angeles Raiders all had strong seasons, proving that they still had plenty of gas left in the tank.

Super Bowl XIX

Super Bowl XIX was the championship game of the 1984 NFL season, played on January 20, 1985, at Stanford Stadium in Stanford, California. The game featured the Miami Dolphins, who were making their fourth Super Bowl appearance in franchise history, and the San Francisco 49ers, who were making their second Super Bowl appearance.

The game was a highly anticipated matchup between two of the best teams in the NFL that year, and it did not disappoint. The 49ers struck first with a 33-yard touchdown pass from quarterback Joe Montana to wide receiver Carl Monroe, but the Dolphins responded with a 1-yard touchdown run by running back Woody Bennett. The 49ers took the lead again in the second quarter with a 14-yard touchdown pass from Montana to tight end John Frank, but the Dolphins tied the game at 10-10 just before halftime with a 30-yard field goal by kicker Uwe von Schamann.

In the second half, the 49ers took control of the game, with Montana leading the way with his precise passing and scrambling ability. Montana threw touchdown passes to wide receiver Freddie Solomon and running back Roger Craig in the third quarter, giving the 49ers a 28-10 lead.

The Dolphins mounted a comeback in the fourth quarter, with quarterback Dan Marino throwing two touchdown passes to wide receiver Mark Clayton. However, it was too little too late, as the 49ers held on to win the game 38-16.

Montana was named the game's Most Valuable Player, completing 24 of 35 passes for 331 yards and three touchdowns. Craig also had a standout performance, rushing for 58 yards and a touchdown on 15 carries, and catching seven passes for 77 yards and a touchdown.

Super Bowl XIX was a historic game for the 49ers, as they won their second Super Bowl in franchise history and cemented their status as one of the best teams of the 1980s. It was also a memorable moment for Montana, who proved himself to be one of the best quarterbacks in NFL history with his outstanding performance in the game.

Overall, Super Bowl XIX was a thrilling and exciting game that provided fans with plenty of entertainment and drama. It was a fitting end to the 1984 NFL season, and it set the stage for even more unforgettable Super Bowls in the years to come.

The 1984 NFL season was a year of historic performances, dominant teams, and iconic players. The introduction of the 2-point conversion and the retirement of Terry Bradshaw marked important changes for the league. Players like Dan Marino and Jerry Rice had historic seasons, while the dominance of the San Francisco 49ers and the resurgence of iconic players reminded fans that the NFL is a league of constant change and evolution. Overall, the 1984 season was one of the most exciting and memorable seasons in NFL history.

1985

The 1985 NFL season was a year of both highs and lows. While the league saw some impressive performances by individual players and teams, it also faced some significant controversies and tragedies.

Key Events

One of the most significant events of the 1985 NFL season was the Chicago Bears' dominant run to the Super Bowl. The Bears finished the regular season with a 15-1 record and a historically dominant defense led by linebacker Mike

Singletary. The Bears' Super Bowl victory over the New England Patriots cemented their place in NFL history.

Another important event of the 1985 season was the signing of the league's first collective bargaining agreement (CBA). The CBA provided players with more rights and protections and established a salary cap for the first time in NFL history.

Players

The 1985 NFL season featured several notable players, including some of the league's biggest stars. One of the most significant players from this season was San Francisco 49ers quarterback Joe Montana. Montana threw for 3,653 yards and 27 touchdowns during the season, leading the 49ers to a 10-6 record and a playoff berth.

Another standout player from the 1985 season was Miami Dolphins quarterback Dan Marino. Marino threw for 4,137 yards and 30 touchdowns during the season, leading the Dolphins to a 12-4 record and a playoff appearance.

Storylines

One of the most significant storylines from the 1985 season was the tragedy that occurred during a game between the New York Giants and the Washington Redskins. Giants linebacker Lawrence Taylor tackled Redskins quarterback Joe Theismann, causing a gruesome leg injury that ended Theismann's career. The incident remains one of the most memorable and tragic moments in NFL history.

Another significant storyline from the 1985 season was the controversy surrounding the use of steroids in the league. The league began implementing drug testing policies in

1985, and several players were suspended for violating the policy.

Super Bowl XX

Super Bowl XX was the championship game of the 1985 NFL season, played on January 26, 1986, at the Louisiana Superdome in New Orleans, Louisiana. The game featured the Chicago Bears, who were making their first Super Bowl appearance in franchise history, and the New England Patriots, who were making their first Super Bowl appearance as well.

The game was a one-sided affair, with the Bears dominating from start to finish. The Bears got off to a quick start with a 28-yard touchdown pass from quarterback Jim McMahon to wide receiver Willie Gault in the first quarter. They extended their lead to 23-3 by halftime, with two field goals by kicker Kevin Butler and a 1-yard touchdown run by fullback Matt Suhey.

In the second half, the Bears continued to dominate, with McMahon throwing two more touchdown passes to tight end Emery Moorehead and running back Walter Payton. The Bears' defense also put on a spectacular performance, intercepting Patriots quarterback Tony Eason three times and sacking him seven times.

The Patriots managed to score a touchdown in the fourth quarter on a 1-yard run by running back Craig James, but it was too little too late. The Bears went on to win the game 46-10, with McMahon being named the game's Most Valuable Player after completing 12 of 20 passes for 256 yards and two touchdowns.

Super Bowl XX was a historic game for the Bears, as they became one of the most dominant teams in NFL history with their crushing victory. The Bears' defense, led by players like defensive end Richard Dent and linebacker Mike Singletary, set a Super Bowl record with seven sacks and held the Patriots to just 123 yards of total offense.

The game was also a memorable moment for Payton, who finally won a Super Bowl in the twilight of his legendary career. The game was a fitting end to the 1985 NFL season, and it set the stage for even more memorable Super Bowls in the years to come.

The 1985 NFL season was a year of both triumph and tragedy. The dominant play of the Chicago Bears and the stellar performances of players like Joe Montana and Dan Marino made for some memorable moments on the field. However, the tragic injury to Joe Theismann and the controversy surrounding the use of steroids served as stark reminders of the dangers and challenges facing the NFL. Ultimately, the 1985 season remains an important chapter in NFL history, highlighting the need for continued evolution and improvement in the sport.

1986

The NFL in 1986 was a year of contrasts. On one hand, the league was riding high on the popularity of the previous year's Super Bowl between the Chicago Bears and the New England Patriots. On the other hand, the league faced controversy with the ongoing player strike that threatened to cancel games and disrupt the season.

The Player Strike: A Clash of Interests

The 1986 NFL player strike was a turning point in the history of the league. It lasted for 24 days, during which time the players sought better pay, benefits, and working conditions. The dispute highlighted the tensions between the players and the league owners, and ultimately resulted in a compromise that laid the foundation for future negotiations. In this section, we will take a closer look at the 1986 player strike, examining the causes, consequences, and significance of this landmark event.

Causes of the Strike: The 1986 player strike was the result of long-standing tensions between the players and the league owners. The players sought a greater share of the league's revenues, as well as better working conditions and benefits. They also wanted to reduce the restrictions on free agency, which would allow players to negotiate contracts with other teams after their contracts expired. The league owners, however, were reluctant to grant these demands, as they feared that it would lead to an escalation in player salaries and reduce their profits.

Consequences of the Strike: The 1986 player strike had several significant consequences. First, it led to the cancellation of one game and the rescheduling of seven others, disrupting the season and alienating fans. Second, it highlighted the power dynamics between the players and the league owners, with the players demonstrating their ability to withhold their labor and force concessions. Third, it laid the foundation for future negotiations between the players and the league, as the two sides were forced to come to a compromise to end the strike.

The Compromise: The 1986 player strike was ultimately resolved on October 15, 1986, when the players agreed to return to work under the previous agreement, while negotiations continued. The compromise included several concessions from the league owners, including an increase in player salaries and benefits, and a reduction in the restrictions on free agency. While the compromise did not satisfy all of the players' demands, it represented a significant step forward in their ongoing negotiations with the league.

Significance of the Strike: The 1986 player strike was a significant event in the history of the NFL. It highlighted the tensions between the players and the league owners, and demonstrated the power of collective bargaining in securing concessions. It also set the stage for future negotiations between the players and the league, as they continued to seek better pay, benefits, and working conditions. The strike was a reminder that the NFL was not just a game, but also a business, and that the interests of the players and the league owners were often in conflict.

The 1986 NFL player strike was a landmark event in the history of the league. It demonstrated the power of collective bargaining, and highlighted the tensions between the players and the league owners. While the strike disrupted the season and alienated fans, it ultimately led to a compromise that laid the foundation for future negotiations between the players and the league. The strike was a reminder that the NFL was not just a game, but also a business, and that the interests of the players and the league owners were often in conflict.

The New York Giants

The New York Giants emerged as one of the top teams in the league in 1986, led by head coach Bill Parcells and quarterback Phil Simms. The Giants finished the season with a 14-2 record, and Simms had a breakout year, throwing for 3,487 yards and 21 touchdowns. The Giants' defense, led by linebacker Lawrence Taylor, was also dominant, allowing the fewest points in the league.

The Denver Broncos

The Denver Broncos were another team that had a successful season in 1986. Led by quarterback John Elway and running back Sammy Winder, the Broncos finished with an 11-5 record and won the AFC West division. In the playoffs, the Broncos defeated the New England Patriots and Cleveland Browns before losing to the Giants in Super Bowl XXI.

Individual Performances

Several players had standout seasons in 1986. Quarterback Dan Marino of the Miami Dolphins threw for 4,746 yards and 44 touchdowns, breaking several records. Running back Eric Dickerson of the Los Angeles Rams rushed for 1,821 yards, leading the league in rushing for the third consecutive year. Wide receiver Jerry Rice of the San Francisco 49ers caught 86 passes for 1,570 yards and 15 touchdowns, establishing himself as one of the best receivers in the league.

The Super Bowl Shuffle

One of the highlights of the 1985 season was the Chicago Bears' "Super Bowl Shuffle" music video, which featured several players rapping and dancing. The video became a pop culture phenomenon, and the Bears went on to win the Super Bowl that year. In 1986, the Bears tried to repeat their success, but their season ended in disappointment as they lost in the divisional round of the playoffs to the Washington Redskins.

Super Bowl XXI

Super Bowl XXI was the championship game of the 1986 NFL season, played on January 25, 1987, at the Rose Bowl in Pasadena, California. The game featured the Denver Broncos, who were making their second Super Bowl appearance in franchise history, and the New York Giants, who were making their first Super Bowl appearance in 18 years.

The game started off slow, with both teams struggling to get on the scoreboard in the first quarter. However, the Giants got going in the second quarter, with quarterback Phil Simms throwing a 6-yard touchdown pass to tight end Zeke Mowatt to give the Giants a 7-0 lead. The Broncos responded with a 48-yard field goal by kicker Rich Karlis, but the Giants extended their lead to 14-3 just before halftime with a 13-yard touchdown pass from Simms to wide receiver Phil McConkey.

In the second half, the Giants took control of the game, with Simms putting on a masterful performance. Simms threw two more touchdown passes to wide receiver Mark Bavaro and running back Joe Morris, and the Giants' defense shut down the Broncos' offense.

The Broncos managed to score a touchdown in the fourth quarter on a 47-yard pass from quarterback John Elway to wide receiver Steve Sewell, but it was too little too late. The Giants went on to win the game 39-20, with Simms being named the game's Most Valuable Player after completing 22 of 25 passes for 268 yards and three touchdowns.

Super Bowl XXI was a historic game for the Giants, as they won their first Super Bowl in franchise history and established themselves as one of the best teams in the NFL. The game was also a memorable moment for Simms, who proved himself to be one of the best quarterbacks in the league with his outstanding performance in the game.

Overall, Super Bowl XXI was a thrilling and exciting game that provided fans with plenty of entertainment and drama. It was a fitting end to the 1986 NFL season, and it set the stage for even more unforgettable Super Bowls in the years to come.

The NFL in 1986 was a year of contrasts, with the excitement of the previous year's Super Bowl and the disappointment of the player strike. The New York Giants emerged as the top team in the league, while several players had standout seasons. The season set the stage for the NFL to continue its growth in popularity and become a dominant force in American sports.

1987

The 1987 NFL season was a unique one, as it was almost cancelled due to a player strike. The strike lasted for 24 days, resulting in the cancellation of one game and the rescheduling of others. However, the league was able to salvage the season by playing with replacement players. In this section, we will take a closer look at the 1987 NFL season, examining the impact of the player strike and the use of replacement players.

The Player Strike

The 1987 NFL player strike was the second in as many years, as the players continued to seek better pay, benefits, and working conditions. The strike lasted from September 22 to October 15, resulting in the cancellation of one game and the rescheduling of others. The players were able to secure some concessions from the league owners, including an increase in the minimum salary and a reduction in the restrictions on free agency.

The Use of Replacement Players

With the player strike ongoing, the league owners decided to use replacement players to salvage the season. These players were mostly former college players, arena football players, and others who were not affiliated with the NFL. The use of replacement players was controversial, as it was seen as undermining the integrity of the league and the quality of play. However, the replacement players were able to keep the season going, and some even made an impact on their teams.

Impact of the Strike and Replacement Players

The 1987 NFL season was marked by a player strike that lasted for 24 days, resulting in the cancellation of one game and the rescheduling of others. In response, the league owners decided to use replacement players to salvage the season.

The Impact on the League: The 1987 NFL strike had a significant impact on the league, as it disrupted the season and created tension between the players and the league owners. The strike also highlighted the need for a better collective bargaining agreement between the two sides. The use of replacement players was seen as a way for the league owners to undermine the players' bargaining power and to show that they could play games without the star players. However, the use of replacement players also created a divide within the league, as some players crossed the picket lines to play, while others refused to do so.

The Impact on the Players: The 1987 NFL strike had a significant impact on the players, as it created tension within the locker room and led to some players crossing the picket line to play as replacement players. The use of replacement players was seen as a way for the league owners to break the players' solidarity and to show that they could play games without the star players. Some players saw this as a betrayal of their union and their fellow players. The use of replacement players also put the players' safety at risk, as the replacement players were not as experienced or trained as the regular players.

The Impact on the Fans: The 1987 NFL strike had a significant impact on the fans, as it disrupted the season and alienated some fans. The cancellation of one game and the rescheduling of others caused confusion and frustration among fans, who were already dealing with the aftermath of the 1986 NFL player strike. The use of replacement players also raised concerns about the quality of play and the integrity of the league. Some fans saw the use of replacement players as a cheapening of the product, and refused to support the league until the regular players returned.

The 1987 NFL strike and the use of replacement players had a significant impact on the league, the players, and the fans. The strike disrupted the season and created tension between the players and the league owners. The use of replacement players was seen as a way for the league owners to undermine the players' bargaining power and to show that they could play games without the star players. However, the use of replacement players also put the players' safety at risk and alienated some fans. The 1987 NFL season was a reminder of the importance of labor relations in professional sports, and of the need for a better collective bargaining agreement between the players and the league owners.

Super Bowl XXII

Despite the disruptions caused by the player strike and the use of replacement players, the 1987 NFL season culminated in a thrilling Super Bowl.

Super Bowl XXII was played on January 31, 1988, at Jack Murphy Stadium in San Diego, California. The game featured the Denver Broncos, who were making their third Super Bowl appearance in four years, and the Washington Redskins, who were making their third Super Bowl appearance in franchise history.

The game started off well for the Broncos, with quarterback John Elway leading the team to an early 10-0 lead with a touchdown pass to running back Ricky Nattiel and a field goal by kicker Rich Karlis. However, the Redskins responded in a big way in the second quarter, scoring 35 points and setting a Super Bowl record for most points scored in a single quarter.

The Redskins' offense was led by quarterback Doug Williams, who threw four touchdown passes in the quarter, including two to wide receiver Ricky Sanders and one each to wide receivers Gary Clark and Clint Didier. The Redskins' defense also put on a strong performance, intercepting Elway three times and holding the Broncos to just 10 yards rushing in the game.

The Broncos managed to score a touchdown in the third quarter on a 56-yard pass from Elway to wide receiver Vance Johnson, but it was too little too late. The Redskins went on to win the game 42-10, with Williams being named the game's Most Valuable Player after completing 18 of 29 passes for 340 yards and four touchdowns.

Super Bowl XXII was a historic game for the Redskins, as they won their second Super Bowl in franchise history and established themselves as one of the best teams in the NFL. The game was also a memorable moment for Williams, who became the first African American quarterback to start in a Super Bowl and led his team to a dominant victory.

Overall, Super Bowl XXII was a thrilling and exciting game that provided fans with plenty of entertainment and drama. It was a fitting end to the 1987 NFL season, and it set the stage for even more unforgettable Super Bowls in the years to come.

The 1987 NFL season was a unique one, marked by a player strike and the use of replacement players. While the strike disrupted the season and raised concerns about the quality of play, the league was able to salvage the season and culminate in a thrilling Super Bowl. The use of replacement players was controversial, but it provided an opportunity for some players to showcase their talent and potentially earn a spot on an NFL roster. The 1987 NFL season was a reminder that the league was not immune to labor disputes, and that the interests of the players and the league owners were often in conflict.

1988: A Year of Comebacks and Dominance

The 1988 NFL season was marked by several notable comebacks and dominant performances by some of the league's top teams and players.

The Comebacks

One of the most memorable comebacks of the 1988 NFL season was orchestrated by the Buffalo Bills in their game against the Houston Oilers on January 3, 1988. The Bills were down by 32 points in the second half, but rallied to score 35 unanswered points and win the game 41-38 in overtime. This game is still known as "The Comeback" and is considered one of the greatest comebacks in NFL history.

Joe Montana's Return to the San Francisco 49ers in 1988

Joe Montana was one of the greatest quarterbacks in NFL history, leading the San Francisco 49ers to four Super Bowl victories in the 1980s. However, his career was almost derailed by a serious back injury that forced him to miss most of the 1986 and 1987 seasons.

The Injury: Montana suffered a serious back injury in the 1986 season opener against the Tampa Bay Buccaneers. He missed the next eight games before returning in Week 10 against the St. Louis Cardinals. However, Montana re-injured his back in that game and was forced to miss the rest of the season.

Montana attempted to come back in 1987, but his back continued to bother him and he played in only one game, a loss to the Los Angeles Rams in Week 3.

The Return: Montana's return to the 49ers in 1988 was eagerly anticipated by fans and pundits alike. There were doubts about whether he would be able to regain his old form after two years away from the game and a serious injury. However, Montana was determined to come back and worked hard during the offseason to get himself ready.

Montana's first game back was in Week 3 of the 1988 season against the Philadelphia Eagles. He completed 15 of 26 passes for 186 yards and one touchdown in a 38-28 victory. Montana's return to form was a major boost for the 49ers, who went on to win their next four games.

Impact on the Team: Montana's return had a major impact on the 49ers, who went on to finish the season with a 10-6 record and a playoff berth. Montana threw for 2,613 yards and 18 touchdowns in 13 games, and was named to the Pro Bowl for the sixth time in his career. His leadership and experience were invaluable to the team, as he guided them through some tough games and critical situations.

The 49ers advanced to the NFC Championship game, where they faced the Minnesota Vikings. Montana threw for 458 yards and three touchdowns in the game, leading the 49ers to Super Bowl XXIII.

Impact on the League: Montana's return to the NFL was not only important for the 49ers, but also for the league as a whole. He was one of the most popular and successful players of his era, and his comeback after a serious injury was seen as a symbol of resilience and determination.

Montana's return also helped to raise the profile of the NFL and attract more fans to the game. His performances on the field were a testament to his skill and talent, and he continued to be a major star in the league for several more years.

Joe Montana's return to the San Francisco 49ers in 1988 was a major event in the history of the NFL. His comeback after a serious injury was a testament to his determination and resilience, and his performances on the field were a major boost for the 49ers and the league as a whole. Montana's impact on the game of football is still felt today, and his return in 1988 will always be remembered as one of the great moments in NFL history.

Dominant Performances

The 1988 NFL season was also marked by dominant performances by some of the league's top teams and players. The Cincinnati Bengals finished the regular season with a 12-4 record and won the AFC Central division. Led by quarterback Boomer Esiason and running back Ickey Woods, the Bengals advanced to Super Bowl XXIII, where they lost to the San Francisco 49ers in a close game.

Another dominant team of the 1988 season was the Minnesota Vikings, who finished the regular season with an 11-5 record and won the NFC Central division. Led by quarterback Wade Wilson and wide receiver Anthony Carter, the Vikings advanced to the NFC Championship game, where they lost to the eventual Super Bowl champions, the San Francisco 49ers.

Individual standout performances of the 1988 season included running back Eric Dickerson of the Indianapolis Colts, who rushed for 1,659 yards and 14 touchdowns, and linebacker Mike Singletary of the Chicago Bears, who was named the NFL Defensive Player of the Year.

Super Bowl XXIII

Super Bowl XXIII was the championship game of the 1988 NFL season, played on January 22, 1989, at Joe Robbie Stadium in Miami, Florida. The game featured the Cincinnati Bengals, who were making their second Super Bowl appearance in franchise history, and the San Francisco 49ers, who were making their third Super Bowl appearance in franchise history.

The game was a closely contested affair, with both teams struggling to get on the scoreboard in the first half. The 49ers managed to take a 3-0 lead on a field goal by kicker Mike Cofer, but the Bengals responded with a touchdown pass from quarterback Boomer Esiason to tight end Rodney Holman to take a 7-3 lead.

In the second half, the 49ers took control of the game, with quarterback Joe Montana putting on a masterful performance. Montana threw two touchdown passes to wide receiver Jerry Rice, including a 10-yard pass with just 34 seconds left in the game to give the 49ers a 20-16 lead.

The Bengals had one last chance to win the game, but their final drive fell short, with a potential game-winning touchdown pass batted down in the end zone. The 49ers went on to win the game 20-16, with Montana being named the game's Most Valuable Player after completing 23 of 36 passes for 357 yards and two touchdowns.

Super Bowl XXIII was a historic game for the 49ers, as they won their third Super Bowl in franchise history and established themselves as one of the best teams in the NFL. The game was also a memorable moment for Montana and Rice, who cemented their status as one of the greatest quarterback-wide receiver duos in NFL history with their performance in the game.

Overall, Super Bowl XXIII was a thrilling and exciting game that provided fans with plenty of entertainment and drama. It was a fitting end to the 1988 NFL season, and it set the stage for even more unforgettable Super Bowls in the years to come.

The 1988 NFL season was a year of comebacks and dominance, as several teams and players rose to the top of the league. The Buffalo Bills' historic comeback against the Houston Oilers, the return of Joe Montana to the San Francisco 49ers, and the dominant performances of the Cincinnati Bengals and Minnesota Vikings were some of the highlights of the season. Individual standout performances by players like Eric Dickerson and Mike Singletary also added to the excitement of the season. The 1988 NFL season remains a memorable year in the league's history.

1989

The NFL in the year 1989 was an exciting time for American football enthusiasts. The league consisted of 28 teams and had just celebrated its 70th anniversary. This section will provide an overview of the NFL in 1989, including key events, important players, and notable moments.

The NFL in 1989

The NFL in 1989 was dominated by the San Francisco 49ers, who won their second consecutive Super Bowl championship. Led by Hall of Fame quarterback Joe Montana and head coach Bill Walsh, the 49ers finished the season with a 14-2 record, earning them the top seed in the playoffs.

Other notable teams in 1989 included the Denver Broncos, who finished the season with an 11-5 record and advanced to the playoffs, and the Buffalo Bills, who finished with a 9-7 record but missed the playoffs. The Cleveland Browns also had a strong season, finishing with a 9-6-1 record, but lost to the Broncos in the AFC Championship game.

Notable Players

Joe Montana was undoubtedly the most dominant player in the NFL in 1989. He threw for 3,521 yards and 26 touchdowns, earning him his third Super Bowl MVP award. Other notable quarterbacks included Dan Marino of the Miami Dolphins and Jim Everett of the Los Angeles Rams, who both threw for over 3,900 yards and 20 touchdowns.

The league's top running back in 1989 was Barry Sanders of the Detroit Lions. Sanders rushed for 1,470 yards and 14 touchdowns, earning him Offensive Rookie of the Year honors. Other notable running backs included Christian

Okoye of the Kansas City Chiefs and Thurman Thomas of the Buffalo Bills.

On the defensive side of the ball, Lawrence Taylor of the New York Giants was still dominant, recording 15.5 sacks and earning Defensive Player of the Year honors. Other standout defenders included Derrick Thomas of the Kansas City Chiefs and Bruce Smith of the Buffalo Bills.

Notable Moments

One of the most memorable moments of the 1989 NFL season was "The Drive II," a game-winning drive by John Elway and the Denver Broncos in the AFC Championship game against the Cleveland Browns. Trailing 21-3 in the third quarter, Elway led the Broncos on a 98-yard touchdown drive and a game-tying two-point conversion. In overtime, the Broncos won on a field goal, advancing to Super Bowl XXIV.

Another notable moment was the retirement of Tom Landry, the longtime head coach of the Dallas Cowboys. Landry had been the Cowboys' head coach since the team's inception in 1960 and had led the team to two Super Bowl victories. His retirement marked the end of an era in Dallas.

Super Bowl XXIV

Super Bowl XXIV was the championship game of the 1989 NFL season, played on January 28, 1990, at the Louisiana Superdome in New Orleans, Louisiana. The game featured the San Francisco 49ers, who were making their fourth Super Bowl appearance in franchise history, and the Denver Broncos, who were making their third Super Bowl appearance in four years.

The game was a complete domination by the 49ers, who set several Super Bowl records en route to a 55-10 victory. The 49ers' offense was led by quarterback Joe Montana, who threw for 297 yards and five touchdowns in the game, both Super Bowl records at the time. Wide receiver Jerry Rice also set a Super Bowl record with 215 receiving yards and a touchdown.

The 49ers' defense was equally impressive, intercepting Broncos quarterback John Elway twice and holding the Broncos to just 167 total yards of offense. The 49ers' 55 points scored in the game remain the most ever scored in a Super Bowl, and the 45-point margin of victory remains the second-largest in Super Bowl history.

The 49ers' dominant performance in Super Bowl XXIV cemented their status as one of the greatest teams in NFL history, and it was a fitting end to a season in which they finished with a 14-2 record and dominated the league from start to finish.

Super Bowl XXIV was also a memorable moment for Montana and Rice, who further established themselves as two of the greatest players in NFL history with their performance in the game. Montana was named the game's Most Valuable Player for the third time in his career, tying a record held by Pittsburgh Steelers quarterback Terry Bradshaw.

Overall, Super Bowl XXIV was a one-sided affair, but it provided fans with plenty of entertainment and excitement. It was a fitting end to the 1989 NFL season, and it set the stage for even more unforgettable Super Bowls in the years to come.

The NFL in 1989 was an exciting time for American football enthusiasts. The San Francisco 49ers were dominant, Joe Montana was at his peak, and there were many other standout players and notable moments. Fans of the game will always remember the 1989 season as a great time for the NFL.

THE 1990'S

1990

The NFL in 1990 was a time of significant change and progress. The league was expanding, with new teams joining the ranks, and the game was evolving, with new rules being implemented to make the sport safer and more entertaining.

This section will explore some of the key developments in the NFL during the year 1990, including the addition of two new teams, the implementation of new rules, and the rise of some of the league's top players.

Expansion

The year 1990 saw the addition of two new teams to the NFL, the Jacksonville Jaguars and the Carolina Panthers. These new teams brought the total number of teams in the league to 28 and created a new division, the AFC South, to accommodate the Jaguars. The addition of these new teams not only expanded the league's reach but also created more opportunities for players and coaches to showcase their skills and strategies.

Rule Changes

The NFL in 1990 also saw significant rule changes that impacted how the game was played. One of the most notable changes was the implementation of the "in the grasp" rule, which allowed quarterbacks to be considered "down" even if they were not tackled to the ground, but rather held by a defender. This rule was designed to protect quarterbacks from injury and reduce the number of unnecessary hits they took during a game.

Another significant rule change in 1990 was the expansion of instant replay review. Replay had been used since 1986 but was only used to review certain types of calls. In 1990, the NFL expanded the use of instant replay to include reviews of touchdowns, turnovers, and certain other types of calls. This change was designed to improve the accuracy of game calls and reduce the potential for errors.

Top Players

1990 was a year that saw many players rise to the top of the NFL. Some of the most notable players that year included quarterback Joe Montana of the San Francisco 49ers, who led his team to victory in Super Bowl XXIV and was named the game's Most Valuable Player. Running back Barry Sanders of the Detroit Lions was also a standout player, earning the NFL's Offensive Rookie of the Year award and rushing for over 1,300 yards in his first season. Other top players that year included quarterback Warren Moon of the Houston Oilers, receiver Jerry Rice of the San Francisco 49ers, and linebacker Lawrence Taylor of the New York Giants.

Super Bowl XXV

Super Bowl XXV was the championship game of the 1990 NFL season, played on January 27, 1991, at Tampa Stadium in Tampa, Florida. The game featured the Buffalo Bills, who were making their first Super Bowl appearance in franchise history, and the New York Giants, who were making their second Super Bowl appearance in five years.

The game was a closely contested affair, with both teams trading blows throughout the game. The Giants took an early lead on a field goal by kicker Matt Bahr, but the Bills responded with a touchdown pass from quarterback Jim Kelly to wide receiver Andre Reed to take a 7-3 lead.

In the second half, the Giants took control of the game, with their defense putting on a dominant performance. The Giants' defense, led by linebacker Lawrence Taylor, held the Bills' high-powered offense to just 19 points, well below their season average of 29.5 points per game.

With the game tied at 20-20 in the final minutes, the Giants mounted a 14-play, 75-yard drive that took nearly nine minutes off the clock. The drive culminated in a 21-yard field goal by Bahr with just four seconds left in the game, giving the Giants a 23-20 victory.

One of the most iconic moments was the "Wide Right" missed field goal by Buffalo Bills kicker Scott Norwood, which ultimately cost the Bills the championship. The moment has since become a symbol of both the agony of defeat and the resilience of the human spirit.

The game was a historic moment for the Giants, who won their second Super Bowl in franchise history and established themselves as one of the best teams in the NFL. The game was also a memorable moment for quarterback Jeff Hostetler, who had taken over for injured starter Phil Simms earlier in the season and led the Giants to victory in the Super Bowl.

Super Bowl XXV was also notable for its pregame festivities, which included a stirring rendition of the national anthem by Whitney Houston. Houston's performance, which has since become iconic, set the stage for a memorable and exciting Super Bowl that provided fans with plenty of drama and excitement.

Overall, Super Bowl XXV was a thrilling and closely contested game that provided fans with plenty of entertainment and excitement. It was a fitting end to the 1990 NFL season, and it set the stage for even more unforgettable Super Bowls in the years to come.

The NFL in 1990 was a year of significant change and progress. With the addition of two new teams and the implementation of new rules, the league was expanding and evolving. This year also saw the rise of some of the league's top players, who would go on to become legends of the sport. As the NFL continued to grow and change, 1990 would be remembered as a year of innovation and advancement in professional football.

1991

The year 1991 was an exciting time for the NFL, as several dominant teams emerged and memorable moments were created. Let's explore some of the key developments in the NFL during the year 1991, including the rise of dominant teams, the performance of standout players, and some of the most memorable moments of the season.

Dominant Teams

In 1991, several NFL teams emerged as dominant forces on the field. One of the most notable was the Washington Redskins, who finished the regular season with a record of 14-2 and went on to Super Bowl XXVI. Led by quarterback Mark Rypien and a powerful offense, the Redskins dominated opponents throughout the season and cemented their place as one of the greatest teams in NFL history.

Another dominant team in 1991 was the Buffalo Bills, who finished the regular season with a record of 13-3 and advanced to their second consecutive Super Bowl. Despite ultimately falling short in the championship game, the Bills showcased their talent and resilience throughout the season, led by quarterback Jim Kelly and a high-powered offense.

Standout Players

1991 was also a year that saw many standout players rise to the top of the NFL. One of the most notable was Detroit Lions running back Barry Sanders, who rushed for over 1,500 yards and earned the NFL's Most Valuable Player award. Sanders' dynamic running style and explosive playmaking ability made him one of the most exciting players in the league, and he continued to impress throughout his career.

Another standout player in 1991 was San Francisco 49ers quarterback Steve Young, who threw for over 3,500 yards and led his team to the NFC Championship game. Young's athleticism and accuracy were on full display throughout the season, earning him widespread recognition as one of the league's top quarterbacks.

Memorable Moments

Another memorable moment in 1991 was the "Monday Night Miracle" game between the Denver Broncos and the Kansas City Chiefs, which featured a record-breaking performance by Broncos quarterback John Elway. In the game, Elway led his team back from a 24-point deficit in the second half, ultimately winning the game in overtime and solidifying his place as one of the greatest quarterbacks in NFL history.

Super Bowl XXVI

Super Bowl XXVI was the championship game of the 1991 NFL season, played on January 26, 1992, at the Metrodome in Minneapolis, Minnesota. The game featured the Washington Redskins, who were making their third Super Bowl appearance in franchise history, and the Buffalo Bills, who were making their second consecutive Super Bowl appearance and hoping to avenge their loss in the previous year's game.

The Redskins dominated the game from start to finish, with their high-powered offense and suffocating defense overwhelming the Bills. The Redskins' offense, led by quarterback Mark Rypien, scored early and often, with Rypien throwing for 292 yards and two touchdowns in the game.

The Redskins' defense was equally impressive, intercepting Bills quarterback Jim Kelly four times and holding the Bills to just 13 points. The Bills' high-powered offense, which had scored an NFL-record 639 points in the regular season, was completely shut down by the Redskins' defense.

The game was a historic moment for the Redskins, who won their third Super Bowl in franchise history and established themselves as one of the best teams of the early 1990s. The game was also a memorable moment for Rypien, who was named the game's Most Valuable Player after throwing for nearly 300 yards and two touchdowns.

Super Bowl XXVI was also notable for being the first Super Bowl to be held in a cold-weather city with a dome stadium. The Metrodome, which had been completed just six years earlier, provided a climate-controlled environment for the game and ensured that weather would not be a factor.

Overall, Super Bowl XXVI was a dominant performance by the Redskins, who proved to be too much for the Bills to handle. It was a fitting end to the 1991 NFL season, and it set the stage for even more unforgettable Super Bowls in the years to come.

The NFL in 1991 was a year of dominant teams, standout players, and memorable moments. From the dominance of the Washington Redskins and Buffalo Bills to the explosive play of Barry Sanders and Steve Young, the season was filled with excitement and drama. And with unforgettable moments like the "Wide Right" field goal and the "Monday Night Miracle," 1991 will always be remembered as a year of unforgettable moments in NFL history.

1992

The year 1992 brought new stars to the NFL and unpredictable outcomes that kept fans on the edge of their seats. Let's now explore the key developments in the NFL during the year 1992, including the emergence of new stars, the performance of standout players, and some of the most unpredictable moments of the season.

Emerging Stars

In 1992, several young players emerged as stars in the NFL. One of the most notable was Dallas Cowboys quarterback Troy Aikman, who led his team to a 13-3 record and a victory in Super Bowl XXVII. Aikman's strong arm and leadership skills helped him become one of the best quarterbacks of his era, and he continued to lead the Cowboys to success in the years that followed.

Another emerging star in 1992 was San Diego Chargers running back Natrone Means, who rushed for over 1,300 yards and 12 touchdowns in his rookie season. Means' physical running style and ability to break tackles made him a fan favorite, and he would continue to be a force in the NFL for several seasons.

Standout Players

In addition to the emergence of new stars, 1992 also saw many standout players continue to excel. One of the most notable was San Francisco 49ers quarterback Steve Young, who threw for over 3,400 yards and led his team to the NFC Championship game. Young's athleticism and accuracy were on full display, and he cemented his place as one of the top quarterbacks in the NFL.

Another standout player in 1992 was Buffalo Bills running back Thurman Thomas, who rushed for over 1,400 yards and 11 touchdowns. Thomas' versatility and playmaking ability made him a key part of the Bills' offense, and he helped lead them to their third consecutive Super Bowl appearance.

Unpredictable Moments

1992 was also a year that produced several unpredictable outcomes and surprising moments in NFL history. One of the most notable was the "Hail Mary" touchdown pass from Dallas Cowboys quarterback Troy Aikman to wide receiver Michael Irvin in a game against the Minnesota Vikings. The improbable play helped the Cowboys secure a victory and showed the team's resilience and determination.

Another unpredictable moment in 1992 was the upset victory by the Washington Redskins over the previously undefeated Miami Dolphins. The Redskins, who had struggled early in the season, were able to come together and put together a strong performance against one of the best teams in the league.

Super Bowl XXVII

Super Bowl XXVII was the championship game of the 1992 NFL season, played on January 31, 1993, at the Rose Bowl in Pasadena, California. The game featured the Dallas Cowboys, who were making their second Super Bowl appearance in franchise history, and the Buffalo Bills, who were making their third consecutive Super Bowl appearance.

The game was a one-sided affair, with the Cowboys dominating the Bills from start to finish. The Cowboys' high-powered offense, led by quarterback Troy Aikman and running back Emmitt Smith, scored early and often, with Aikman throwing for four touchdowns in the game.

The Cowboys' defense was equally impressive, intercepting Bills quarterback Jim Kelly three times and holding the Bills to just 17 points. The Bills, who had been one of the most dominant teams in the NFL over the previous three seasons, were completely overwhelmed by the Cowboys' dominant performance.

The game was a historic moment for the Cowboys, who won their third Super Bowl in franchise history and established themselves as one of the best teams of the early 1990s. The game was also a memorable moment for Aikman, who was named the game's Most Valuable Player after throwing for four touchdowns and leading the Cowboys to victory.

Super Bowl XXVII was also notable for being the first Super Bowl to feature a halftime show produced by a major pop artist. Michael Jackson performed a memorable halftime show, which included a medley of his greatest hits and a crowd-pleasing rendition of "Billie Jean."

Overall, Super Bowl XXVII was a dominant performance by the Cowboys, who proved to be too much for the Bills to handle. It was a fitting end to the 1992 NFL season, and it set the stage for even more unforgettable Super Bowls in the years to come.

The NFL in 1992 was a year of new stars, standout players, and unpredictable outcomes. From the emergence of Troy Aikman and Natrone Means to the continued excellence of Steve Young and Thurman Thomas, the season was filled with excitement and drama. And with surprising moments like the "Hail Mary" touchdown and the upset victory by the Washington Redskins, 1992 will always be remembered as a year of unpredictability in NFL history.

1993: The Birth of a Dynasty

The year 1993 was a significant one for the NFL, as it marked the beginning of a dynasty that would dominate the league for years to come. This section will explore the key developments in the NFL during the year 1993, including the rise of a new dynasty, standout players, and some of the most memorable moments of the season.

The Birth of a Dynasty

In 1993, the Dallas Cowboys emerged as a dominant force in the NFL, beginning a run of success that would see them win three Super Bowls in four years. Led by head coach Jimmy Johnson and a talented roster that included quarterback Troy Aikman, running back Emmitt Smith, and wide receiver Michael Irvin, the Cowboys finished the regular season with a record of 12-4 and entered the playoffs as one of the top teams in the league.

The Cowboys' dominance continued in the playoffs, as they defeated the Green Bay Packers and San Francisco 49ers to advance to Super Bowl XXVIII. In the Super Bowl, the Cowboys faced the Buffalo Bills for the second consecutive year, and once again emerged victorious, winning 30-13 and securing their second straight Super Bowl championship.

Standout Players

In addition to the rise of the Cowboys as a dominant team, 1993 also saw several standout players continue to excel. One of the most notable was San Francisco 49ers quarterback Steve Young, who threw for over 4,000 yards and led the league with 29 touchdown passes. Young's accuracy and leadership skills helped him win the NFL Most Valuable Player (MVP) award, and he continued to be a force in the league for years to come.

Another standout player in 1993 was Detroit Lions running back Barry Sanders, who rushed for over 1,800 yards and scored 11 touchdowns. Sanders' elusiveness and ability to break tackles made him one of the most exciting players to watch, and he would go on to win the NFL MVP award the following year.

Memorable Moments

1993 was also a year that produced several memorable moments in NFL history. One of the most notable was the "Leon Lett" play in a game between the Cowboys and the Miami Dolphins on Thanksgiving Day. In the closing seconds of the game, Dolphins kicker Pete Stoyanovich attempted a game-winning field goal, but the kick was blocked by the Cowboys. However, Cowboys defensive lineman Leon Lett touched the ball while it was still live, allowing the Dolphins to recover and kick the game-winning field goal on their next play.

Another memorable moment in 1993 was the "Monday Night Miracle" game between the Buffalo Bills and the Houston Oilers. In the game, the Oilers led the Bills by a score of 35-3 at halftime, but the Bills rallied in the second half to score 35 unanswered points and win the game in overtime.

Super Bowl XXVIII

Super Bowl XXVIII was the championship game of the 1993 NFL season, played on January 30, 1994, at the Georgia Dome in Atlanta, Georgia. The game featured the Dallas Cowboys, who were making their second consecutive Super Bowl appearance, and the Buffalo Bills, who were making their fourth consecutive Super Bowl appearance and hoping to finally win the championship after three consecutive losses.

The game was a rematch of the previous year's Super Bowl, and it was another dominant performance by the Cowboys, who once again proved to be too much for the Bills to handle. The Cowboys' offense, led by quarterback Troy Aikman and running back Emmitt Smith, scored early and often, with Smith rushing for 132 yards and two touchdowns in the game.

The Cowboys' defense was equally impressive, intercepting Bills quarterback Jim Kelly three times and holding the Bills to just 13 points. The Bills, who had been one of the most dominant teams in the NFL over the previous four seasons, were completely overwhelmed by the Cowboys' dominant performance.

The game was a historic moment for the Cowboys, who won their fourth Super Bowl in franchise history and solidified their place as one of the greatest teams in NFL history. The game was also a disappointing moment for the Bills, who became the first team in NFL history to lose four consecutive Super Bowls.

Super Bowl XXVIII was also notable for being the first Super Bowl to be played in a domed stadium in the southern United States. The Georgia Dome, which had been completed just two years earlier, provided a climate-controlled environment for the game and ensured that weather would not be a factor.

Overall, Super Bowl XXVIII was another dominant performance by the Cowboys, who proved to be one of the greatest teams in NFL history. It was a fitting end to the 1993 NFL season, and it set the stage for even more unforgettable Super Bowls in the years to come.

The NFL in 1993 was a year of dominance, standout players, and memorable moments. The rise of the Dallas Cowboys as a dominant team and the continued excellence of players like Steve Young and Barry Sanders made for an exciting season, while unforgettable moments like the "Leon Lett" play and the "Monday Night Miracle" added to the drama. And while the Cowboys' dynasty would continue for several more years, 1993 will always be remembered as the year that marked the birth of a new NFL dynasty.

1994

The year 1994 was an exceptional one for the NFL, as it produced some of the greatest performances, players, and moments in the history of the league. Let's now explore the key developments in the NFL during the year 1994, including the emergence of new stars, the dominance of established teams, and some of the most unforgettable moments of the season.

Emerging Stars

In 1994, several young players announced themselves as future stars in the NFL. One of the most notable was Marshall Faulk, a rookie running back for the Indianapolis Colts who rushed for over 1,200 yards and caught 52 passes for another 522 yards. Faulk's versatility and explosiveness made him a force to be reckoned with, and he would go on to become one of the greatest running backs in NFL history.

Another emerging star in 1994 was Brett Favre, the quarterback for the Green Bay Packers. Favre led the Packers to a 9-7 record and a playoff berth, throwing for over 3,300 yards and 19 touchdowns. Favre's gunslinger mentality and fearless approach to the game would make him one of the most beloved players in NFL history, and he would go on to win three MVP awards and a Super Bowl championship.

Established Dominance

In addition to the emergence of new stars, 1994 also saw several established teams continue to dominate the league. The San Francisco 49ers, led by quarterback Steve Young and wide receiver Jerry Rice, finished the regular season with a record of 13-3 and entered the playoffs as one of the top teams in the league. The 49ers' dominance continued in the playoffs, as they defeated the Chicago Bears and Dallas Cowboys to advance to Super Bowl XXIX, where they faced the San Diego Chargers.

In the Super Bowl, the 49ers put on a dominant performance, defeating the Chargers by a score of 49-26.

Steve Young threw for a Super Bowl-record six touchdown passes, while Jerry Rice caught three of those touchdowns and was named the game's MVP. The 49ers' victory cemented their status as one of the greatest teams in NFL history and marked the end of a dominant era in the league.

Memorable Moments

1994 was also a year that produced several unforgettable moments in NFL history. One of the most memorable was the "Heidi Game" between the New York Jets and the Miami Dolphins. In the game, the Jets led the Dolphins by a score of 24-21 with just over a minute remaining, but NBC cut away from the game to show the movie "Heidi." While viewers were watching the movie, the Dolphins scored two touchdowns to win the game, leading to widespread outrage and controversy.

Another memorable moment in 1994 was the "Hail Mary" pass thrown by Green Bay Packers quarterback Brett Favre in a game against the Detroit Lions. With just seconds remaining in the game, Favre threw a desperation pass that was caught by wide receiver Sterling Sharpe for the game-winning touchdown, cementing Favre's status as one of the most clutch players in NFL history.

Super Bowl XXIX

Super Bowl XXIX was the championship game of the 1994 NFL season, played on January 29, 1995, at Joe Robbie Stadium in Miami, Florida. The game featured the San Francisco 49ers, who were making their fifth Super Bowl appearance in franchise history, and the San Diego Chargers, who were making their first Super Bowl appearance in franchise history.

The game was a one-sided affair, with the 49ers dominating the Chargers from start to finish. The 49ers' high-powered offense, led by quarterback Steve Young and wide receiver Jerry Rice, scored early and often, with Young throwing for six touchdowns in the game.

The Chargers' defense, which had been one of the best in the NFL during the regular season, was completely overwhelmed by the 49ers' dominant performance. The Chargers' offense, led by quarterback Stan Humphries, did manage to score 26 points, but it was not enough to keep pace with the 49ers' explosive attack.

The game was a historic moment for the 49ers, who won their fifth Super Bowl in franchise history and established themselves as one of the best teams of the 1990s. The game was also a memorable moment for Young, who was named the game's Most Valuable Player after throwing for six touchdowns and leading the 49ers to victory.

Super Bowl XXIX was also notable for being the first Super Bowl to feature a team from California since Super Bowl XIX in 1985. The game was played in Miami, but it had a distinctly California feel, with both teams hailing from the Golden State.

Overall, Super Bowl XXIX was a dominant performance by the 49ers, who proved to be too much for the Chargers to handle. It was a fitting end to the 1994 NFL season, and it set the stage for even more unforgettable Super Bowls in the years to come.

The NFL in 1994 was a season of greatness, as emerging stars like Marshall Faulk and Brett Favre announced themselves as future legends of the game, while established teams like the San Francisco 49ers continued to dominate.

Memorable moments like the "Heidi Game" and the "Hail Mary" pass added to the drama and excitement of the season, making 1994 one of the greatest years in the history of the National Football League.

1995

The year 1995 was a season of surprises for the NFL, as unexpected teams rose to prominence and established powers faltered. This section will explore the key developments in the NFL during the year 1995, including the emergence of new contenders, the struggles of perennial favorites, and some of the most surprising moments of the season.

Emerging Contenders

In 1995, several teams emerged as surprise contenders in the NFL. One of the most notable was the Carolina Panthers, a second-year expansion team that had struggled in their inaugural season. Under the leadership of head coach Dom Capers and quarterback Kerry Collins, the Panthers finished the season with a record of 7-9 and narrowly missed out on a playoff berth. Despite falling short of the postseason, the Panthers' strong performance in 1995 set the stage for their future success, which would include a Super Bowl appearance just three years later.

Another emerging contender in 1995 was the Indianapolis Colts, who had finished the previous season with a record of 8-8 but had not made the playoffs since 1987. Led by quarterback Jim Harbaugh and running back Marshall Faulk, the Colts finished the season with a record of 9-7 and earned a wild-card berth in the playoffs. Although they were ultimately eliminated in the first round by the Pittsburgh Steelers, the Colts' return to the postseason marked a significant step forward for the franchise.

Struggles of Established Powers

While new contenders emerged in 1995, several established powers faltered. The Dallas Cowboys, who had won three Super Bowls in the previous four years, finished the season with a record of 12-4 but were upset in the divisional round of the playoffs by the upstart Panthers. The San Francisco 49ers, who had won the Super Bowl just one year earlier, also suffered a surprise defeat in the divisional round, losing to the Green Bay Packers by a score of 27-17.

Surprising Moments

1995 was also a year that produced several surprising moments in NFL history. One of the most unexpected was the return of Cleveland Browns owner Art Modell to Baltimore, where he announced his intention to move the Browns franchise to the city and rename it the Baltimore Ravens. The move sparked outrage among Browns fans, who felt betrayed by Modell's decision to abandon the team after 35 years in Cleveland.

Another surprising moment in 1995 was the retirement of legendary quarterback Joe Montana, who had won four Super Bowls with the San Francisco 49ers in the 1980s. Montana, who had been traded to the Kansas City Chiefs in 1993, had struggled with injuries in his final seasons but remained one of the most beloved players in NFL history.

Super Bowl XXX

Super Bowl XXX was the championship game of the 1995 NFL season, played on January 28, 1996, at Sun Devil Stadium in Tempe, Arizona. The game featured the Dallas Cowboys, who were making their third Super Bowl appearance in four years, and the Pittsburgh Steelers, who were making their first Super Bowl appearance since winning Super Bowl XIV in 1980.

The game was a closely contested battle, with both teams playing solid defense and struggling on offense at times. The Cowboys' offense, led by quarterback Troy Aikman and running back Emmitt Smith, managed to score 27 points, but it was their defense that made the biggest impact in the game.

The Cowboys' defense intercepted Steelers quarterback Neil O'Donnell three times, including one interception that was returned for a touchdown by Cowboys cornerback Larry Brown. The interception and touchdown proved to be the turning point in the game, as the Cowboys were able to hold off a late surge by the Steelers to secure the victory.

The game was a historic moment for the Cowboys, who won their fifth Super Bowl in franchise history and became the first team to win three Super Bowls in four years since the San Francisco 49ers in the 1980s. The game was also a disappointing moment for the Steelers, who were hoping to win their fifth Super Bowl in franchise history but were unable to overcome the turnovers and mistakes that plagued them throughout the game.

Super Bowl XXX was also notable for being the first Super Bowl played in a stadium with a retractable roof. Sun Devil Stadium, which had been completed just two years earlier, had a retractable roof that was closed during the game due to rain.

Overall, Super Bowl XXX was a hard-fought battle between two of the NFL's most storied franchises. It was a fitting end to the 1995 NFL season, and it set the stage for even more unforgettable Super Bowls in the years to come.

The NFL in 1995 was a season of surprises, as new contenders emerged, established powers faltered, and unexpected moments shook the league. While the Carolina Panthers and Indianapolis Colts set the stage for their future success, the struggles of the Dallas Cowboys and San Francisco 49ers marked the end of dominant eras in the league. Meanwhile, the controversial move of the Cleveland Browns to Baltimore and the retirement of Joe Montana added to the drama and unpredictability of the season, making 1995 a year that would be remembered for years to come.

1996

The NFL in 1996 marked a significant season of change and dominance. The league saw the emergence of new stars and the downfall of some of its long-standing teams. With the introduction of new rules, technology, and increasing media coverage, the NFL evolved into a more dynamic and exciting game.

The Emergence of Young Stars

The 1996 season saw the emergence of several young stars who would go on to dominate the league for years to come. One such player was Brett Favre, the quarterback of the Green Bay Packers. Favre led his team to an impressive 13-3 record, passing for 3,899 yards and 39 touchdowns, earning him his second consecutive MVP award.

Another standout player was running back Barry Sanders of the Detroit Lions, who rushed for 1,553 yards and 11 touchdowns. Sanders led the league in rushing yards and was named the league's Offensive Player of the Year.

The Downfall of Established Teams

The 1996 season saw the decline of some of the league's most established teams. The Dallas Cowboys, who had won three Super Bowls in the previous four years, finished the season with a disappointing 10-6 record and lost in the divisional round of the playoffs.

The San Francisco 49ers, another dominant team of the 1980s and early 1990s, also struggled, finishing with an 11-5 record but failing to advance beyond the divisional playoffs.

The Rise of the New England Patriots

The New England Patriots had been a struggling franchise for many years prior to the 1996 NFL season. However, in that year, the Patriots emerged as one of the top teams in the league, winning the AFC East division and advancing to the Super Bowl for the first time in franchise history.

The Hiring of Bill Parcells: One of the key factors that contributed to the rise of the Patriots in 1996 was the hiring of Bill Parcells as head coach in 1993. Parcells had a proven track record of success, having led the New York Giants to two Super Bowl victories in the 1980s. Under Parcells' leadership, the Patriots began to build a winning culture and a competitive team.

Drew Bledsoe's Emergence as a Star Quarterback: Another factor that contributed to the rise of the Patriots was the emergence of Drew Bledsoe as a star quarterback. Bledsoe, the first overall pick in the 1993 NFL Draft, had struggled in his first few seasons in the league. However, in 1996, Bledsoe had a breakout season, passing for 4,086 yards and 27 touchdowns, leading the Patriots to an 11-5 record and a division title.

The Strong Performance of the Defense: The Patriots' defense also played a significant role in the team's success in 1996. Led by Pro Bowl linebacker Chris Slade and defensive tackle Chad Eaton, the Patriots' defense was one of the best in the league, allowing only 19.7 points per game. The defense also recorded 37 sacks and 28 turnovers, which helped to keep the team in games and win crucial matches.

Key Wins and Momentum: The Patriots' rise to success in 1996 was also due to key wins and momentum. In Week 3, the Patriots defeated the 2-time defending Super Bowl champion Dallas Cowboys, which was a significant upset and gave the team a boost of confidence. The team also won several close games throughout the season, including a 23-17 victory over the Miami Dolphins in Week 13, which helped to secure the division title.

The rise of the New England Patriots in 1996 was due to a combination of factors. The hiring of Bill Parcells, the emergence of Drew Bledsoe as a star quarterback, the strong performance of the defense, and key wins and momentum all contributed to the team's success. The 1996 season marked the beginning of a new era for the Patriots, one that would see the team become one of the most dominant and successful franchises in NFL history.

Super Bowl XXXI

Super Bowl XXXI was the championship game of the 1996 NFL season, played on January 26, 1997, at the Louisiana Superdome in New Orleans, Louisiana. The game featured the Green Bay Packers, who were making their third Super Bowl appearance in franchise history, and the New England Patriots, who were making their second Super Bowl appearance in franchise history.

The game started out with a bang, as the Packers returned the opening kickoff for a touchdown, setting the tone for a dominant performance. The Packers' high-powered offense, led by quarterback Brett Favre and running back Dorsey Levens, racked up 35 points in the first half alone, putting the game out of reach for the Patriots.

The Patriots' offense, led by quarterback Drew Bledsoe, managed to score 21 points in the game, but it was not enough to keep pace with the Packers' explosive attack. The Packers' defense also played a key role in the game, intercepting Bledsoe four times and sacking him three times.

The game was a historic moment for the Packers, who won their first Super Bowl in 29 years and cemented their place as one of the NFL's most dominant teams of the 1990s. The game was also a disappointing moment for the Patriots, who were unable to overcome the early deficit and were outmatched by the Packers on both sides of the ball.

Super Bowl XXXI was also notable for being the last Super Bowl to be played in the Louisiana Superdome for 10 years. The stadium, which had hosted seven Super Bowls in its history, was damaged by Hurricane Katrina in 2005 and did not host another Super Bowl until Super Bowl XLVII in 2013.

Overall, Super Bowl XXXI was a dominant performance by the Packers, who proved to be too much for the Patriots to handle. It was a fitting end to the 1996 NFL season, and it set the stage for even more unforgettable Super Bowls in the years to come.

The 1996 NFL season was a season of change and dominance. It saw the emergence of new stars, the downfall of established teams, and the rise of new contenders. The season was defined by the dominance of the Green Bay Packers, led by quarterback Brett Favre, who won both the MVP award and the Super Bowl. The 1996 season marked a turning point in the NFL's history, paving the way for a new era of dynamic and exciting football.

1997

The NFL in 1997 was a year of upsets and records. The season saw several surprise teams emerge and break long-standing records. From the Denver Broncos' Super Bowl victory to the Minnesota Vikings' explosive offense, the 1997 season was full of memorable moments. This section explores the significant events, players, and teams that defined the 1997 NFL season.

The Emergence of Upset Teams

The 1997 season saw several surprise teams emerge and challenge the status quo. One such team was the Tampa Bay Buccaneers, who finished with a 10-6 record and made the playoffs for the first time since 1982. The New York Jets, under new head coach Bill Parcells, also surprised many by finishing with a 9-7 record and earning a wild card spot in the playoffs.

The Explosive Offense of the Minnesota Vikings

The Minnesota Vikings' offense in 1997 was one of the most explosive in NFL history. Led by quarterback Randall Cunningham, wide receiver Randy Moss, and running back Robert Smith, the Vikings scored a total of 556 points, breaking the previous record for most points in a season. Despite their offensive prowess, the Vikings were upset in the NFC Championship game by the Atlanta Falcons.

The Record-Breaking Performance of Barry Sanders

Barry Sanders was one of the most electrifying players in NFL history, and his record-breaking performance in 1997 only cemented his legacy as one of the greatest running backs of all time. Sanders had already established himself as one of the best running backs in the league, having rushed for over 1,000 yards in each of his previous eight seasons. However, in 1997, Sanders took his game to another level, breaking one of the most prestigious records in the NFL - Eric Dickerson's single-season rushing record.

Sanders entered the final game of the season needing 131 yards to break Dickerson's record of 2,105 rushing yards in a single season. The Lions were playing against the New York Jets, who had the league's third-ranked run defense. However, Sanders was determined to break the record, and he put on a performance for the ages.

From the opening kickoff, Sanders was in the zone, rushing for 53 yards on his first carry of the game. He continued to pile up yards, breaking tackles and leaving defenders in his wake. With just over two minutes left in the game, Sanders needed just ten yards to break the record. On third down, he took a handoff and burst through a hole in the line, racing down the sideline for a 53-yard touchdown run. The crowd erupted as Sanders was mobbed by his teammates, and he had broken the record in spectacular fashion.

Sanders finished the season with 2,053 rushing yards, becoming the first player in NFL history to rush for over 2,000 yards in a season twice (he had previously done so in 1994). He also became the first player to rush for 1,500 yards or more in five consecutive seasons, further cementing his status as one of the greatest running backs of all time.

Sanders' record-breaking performance in 1997 was a testament to his skill, determination, and sheer athleticism. He proved that he was not just a great running back, but one of the greatest players to ever play the game. Even today, over two decades later, Sanders' record still stands as a testament to his greatness and his impact on the NFL.

Super Bowl XXXII

Super Bowl XXXII was the championship game of the 1997 NFL season, played on January 25, 1998, at Qualcomm Stadium in San Diego, California. The game featured the defending Super Bowl champion Green Bay Packers, who were making their second consecutive Super Bowl appearance, and the Denver Broncos, who were making their fifth Super Bowl appearance in franchise history.

The game was widely anticipated as a matchup between two of the NFL's most dominant quarterbacks: Green Bay's Brett Favre and Denver's John Elway. However, it was the Broncos' running back, Terrell Davis, who stole the show. Davis rushed for 157 yards and three touchdowns, earning him the game's Most Valuable Player award.

The game was a back-and-forth battle, with both teams exchanging blows throughout. The Packers struck first, scoring on a Favre touchdown pass to wide receiver Antonio Freeman. However, the Broncos answered back with a touchdown of their own on a Davis run. The game remained close throughout the first half, with the Packers taking a 17-14 lead into halftime.

In the second half, the Broncos began to pull away, thanks to the dominant running of Davis. He scored two more touchdowns, putting the Broncos up 31-24 with just over three minutes left in the game. The Packers had one last chance to tie the game, but a Favre pass was intercepted in the end zone, sealing the victory for the Broncos.

The win was a historic moment for the Broncos and their quarterback, John Elway, who had previously lost in three Super Bowl appearances. The victory was also a vindication for head coach Mike Shanahan, who had been criticized for his team's failures in the playoffs in previous years.

Super Bowl XXXII was an exciting and memorable game, featuring some of the NFL's biggest stars and showcasing the importance of a dominant running game in championship football. The game set the stage for even more exciting Super Bowls in the years to come, cementing its place as one of the most memorable championship games in NFL history.

The 1997 NFL season was a year of upsets and records. The emergence of surprise teams, the explosive offense of the Minnesota Vikings, the record-breaking performance of Barry Sanders, and the Denver Broncos' Super Bowl victory were all defining moments of the season. The 1997 season demonstrated the unpredictability and excitement of the NFL, and it set the stage for even more memorable moments to come.

1998

The 1998 NFL season will always be remembered as the year of historic offenses. The league saw an explosion in scoring and passing, with several quarterbacks and receivers putting up record-breaking numbers. From the Denver Broncos' repeat Super Bowl victory to the record-setting performances of Randy Moss and Terrell Davis, the 1998 season was full of unforgettable moments.

The Record-Breaking Performance of Randy Moss

Rookie wide receiver Randy Moss was a sensation in his first year in the league, setting a new standard for what a wide receiver could do. Moss quickly became one of the league's most feared deep threats, recording 69 receptions for 1,313 yards and 17 touchdowns. Moss shattered the record for most touchdown receptions by a rookie, and his 17 touchdowns tied the NFL record for most touchdown receptions in a season.

The Dominance of the Denver Broncos

The Denver Broncos had a dominant season in 1998, finishing with a 14-2 record and earning their second straight Super Bowl victory. Led by quarterback John Elway and running back Terrell Davis, the Broncos had the league's top-ranked offense and the second-ranked defense. Davis had a remarkable season, rushing for 2,008 yards and scoring 23 touchdowns. Elway was named the game's MVP, capping off a legendary career.

The Record-Breaking Performance of Terrell Davis

Terrell Davis had one of the most remarkable seasons by a running back in NFL history in 1998. Davis had already established himself as one of the league's top running backs, rushing for over 1,000 yards in each of his first three seasons. However, in 1998, Davis took his game to another level, putting up numbers that few running backs had ever matched.

Davis started the season strong, rushing for over 100 yards in each of the first four games. He continued to pile up yards throughout the season, and by the end of Week 14, he had rushed for 1,697 yards and scored 17 touchdowns. Davis was on pace to break Eric Dickerson's single-season rushing record of 2,105 yards, but he still had three games left to play.

In Week 15, Davis had a monster game against the Miami Dolphins, rushing for 199 yards and two touchdowns. He followed that up with another strong performance against the Detroit Lions, rushing for 157 yards and two touchdowns. With one game left in the season, Davis needed just 154 yards to break Dickerson's record.

In the final game of the season, Davis faced off against the Seattle Seahawks. He wasted no time getting started, rushing for 110 yards in the first half. In the third quarter, Davis broke through for a 15-yard touchdown run, giving him his 23rd rushing touchdown of the season, breaking the previous record of 21. He continued to pile up yards in the fourth quarter, and with just over three minutes left in the game, Davis broke through for a 17-yard run, giving him 2,008 rushing yards on the season and breaking Dickerson's record.

Davis finished the season with 2,008 rushing yards and 21 touchdowns, earning him the NFL's Most Valuable Player award. He had become just the fourth player in NFL history to rush for over 2,000 yards in a season, joining Eric Dickerson, O.J. Simpson, and Barry Sanders. Davis' record-breaking season cemented his legacy as one of the greatest running backs in NFL history and helped lead the Denver Broncos to their second consecutive Super Bowl victory.

Injuries would eventually shorten Davis' career, but his 1998 season remains one of the greatest seasons by a running back in NFL history. His record-breaking performance in 1998 showcased his incredible talent, work ethic, and determination. Today, Davis' record still stands as a testament to his greatness and his impact on the NFL.

The Emergence of Peyton Manning

In 1998, a young quarterback named Peyton Manning burst onto the scene and began what would become one of the most decorated careers in NFL history. After being drafted first overall by the Indianapolis Colts in 1998, Manning quickly showed that he had the talent and work ethic to be a star in the league.

In his rookie season, Manning struggled at times, throwing more interceptions than touchdowns and leading the Colts to a 3-13 record. However, it was clear that Manning had the potential to be a great quarterback. He was a quick learner and a hard worker, constantly studying game film and working with his coaches to improve his game.

In his second season, Manning made significant strides. He threw for over 4,000 yards and 26 touchdowns, leading the Colts to a 13-3 record and a playoff berth. Manning's performance earned him his first Pro Bowl selection, and he was named the NFL's co-MVP (along with Minnesota Vikings quarterback Randall Cunningham).

Over the next several years, Manning continued to establish himself as one of the league's top quarterbacks. He would go on to win five MVP awards (tied for the most in NFL history), make 14 Pro Bowl appearances, and lead the Colts and Denver Broncos to four Super Bowl appearances, winning two of them.

Manning's success was due in part to his remarkable talent as a quarterback. He had a lightning-quick release, great accuracy, and a deep understanding of the game. But it was also due to his work ethic and his dedication to improving his game. Manning was known for his obsessive attention to detail, spending hours each day studying film and working on his technique.

Manning's emergence in 1998 marked the beginning of a new era in the NFL. He would go on to become one of the most beloved and respected players in the league, setting numerous records along the way. But it all started with his breakout season in 1998, when he showed that he had what it takes to be a star in the NFL.

Super Bowl XXXIII

Super Bowl XXXIII was the championship game of the 1998 NFL season, played on January 31, 1999, at Pro Player Stadium in Miami, Florida. The game featured the Denver Broncos, who were making their second consecutive Super Bowl appearance and their sixth in franchise history, and the Atlanta Falcons, who were making their first Super Bowl appearance.

The game was widely anticipated as a battle between two of the NFL's most exciting and dynamic quarterbacks: Denver's John Elway and Atlanta's Chris Chandler. However, it was Elway who once again stole the show, leading the Broncos to a decisive victory and earning his second Super Bowl MVP award.

The game got off to a slow start, with both teams struggling to move the ball and failing to score in the first quarter. However, the Broncos broke through early in the second quarter with a touchdown pass from Elway to tight end Howard Griffith. The Falcons responded with a field goal, but the Broncos quickly extended their lead with another touchdown pass from Elway, this time to wide receiver Rod Smith.

The Falcons scored a touchdown of their own just before halftime to cut the lead to 17-6, but the Broncos continued to dominate in the second half. Elway threw another touchdown pass to Smith, and running back Terrell Davis added two rushing touchdowns to put the game out of reach. The Falcons managed one more touchdown in the fourth quarter, but it was too little, too late, as the Broncos held on for a 34-19 victory.

The win was a historic moment for the Broncos and their quarterback, John Elway, who announced his retirement from the NFL shortly after the game. It was also a testament to the team's dominance throughout the season, finishing with a 14-2 record and winning their last eight games in a row.

Super Bowl XXXIII was an exciting and memorable game, featuring some of the NFL's biggest stars and showcasing the importance of a dominant quarterback in championship football. The game set the stage for even more exciting Super Bowls in the years to come, cementing its place as one of the most memorable championship games in NFL history.

The 1998 NFL season was a year of historic offenses, with record-breaking performances from players like Randy Moss and Terrell Davis. The Denver Broncos' repeat Super Bowl victory and the emergence of Peyton Manning were also defining moments of the season. The 1998 season demonstrated the NFL's ability to evolve and adapt, with offenses becoming more explosive and quarterbacks becoming more important than ever before. The legacy of the 1998 season continues to influence the league today, with teams still striving to put up record-breaking numbers and win championships.

1999

The year 1999 was a significant year for the NFL as it marked the end of the millennium and the start of a new era. The league was still recovering from the labor dispute that resulted in the first work stoppage in its history the previous year. Nevertheless, the NFL was on the cusp of a new era of growth and expansion, with several changes in the horizon.

The Expansion of the League

The most significant development in the NFL in 1999 was the expansion of the league. After years of discussion and planning, the league added two new teams, the Houston Texans, and the Cleveland Browns. The addition of these teams brought the total number of franchises in the NFL to 31, with the league planning to add one more team in the near future.

The return of the Cleveland Browns, a team that had been moved to Baltimore and rebranded as the Ravens in 1996, was especially significant. The move had been controversial and had angered many Cleveland fans. The NFL had promised to bring a team back to Cleveland as soon as possible, and 1999 was the year that promise was fulfilled. The team was rebuilt from scratch and played its first game in the new Cleveland Browns Stadium in September of that year.

On-Field Performances

In terms of on-field performances, the 1999 NFL season was marked by several standout players and teams. The St.

Louis Rams, led by quarterback Kurt Warner and running back Marshall Faulk, had one of the most explosive offenses in league history. The Rams finished the regular season with a 13-3 record and went on to Super Bowl XXXIV.

Another standout player in 1999 was Indianapolis Colts quarterback Peyton Manning. Manning, who was in his second year in the league, threw for over 4,000 yards and 26 touchdowns, establishing himself as one of the best quarterbacks in the NFL. He was named the NFL's Most Valuable Player (MVP) for the 1999 season.

Off-Field Issues

Off-field issues were also a significant part of the NFL in 1999. One of the most notable incidents involved star linebacker Ray Lewis of the Baltimore Ravens. Lewis was charged with murder in connection with an altercation outside a nightclub in Atlanta after the Super Bowl. Lewis was eventually acquitted of the charges, but the incident cast a shadow over the league and highlighted the issue of player behavior off the field.

Another issue that received attention in 1999 was the issue of player safety. Several high-profile injuries occurred during the season, including one to New England Patriots quarterback Drew Bledsoe, who suffered a serious chest injury after being hit by a New York Jets linebacker. The incident led to increased scrutiny of the league's rules and policies regarding player safety.

Super Bowl XXXIV

Super Bowl XXXIV was the championship game of the 1999 NFL season, played on January 30, 2000, at the Georgia Dome in Atlanta, Georgia. The game featured the

Tennessee Titans and the St. Louis Rams, two teams that had surprised many by making it to the big game.

The Rams were led by their dynamic offense, dubbed the "Greatest Show on Turf," which featured quarterback Kurt Warner and a trio of talented wide receivers. The Titans, on the other hand, had made it to the Super Bowl on the strength of their defense and the steady play of quarterback Steve McNair.

The game got off to a slow start, with both teams struggling to score in the first quarter. However, the Rams broke through early in the second quarter with a touchdown pass from Warner to Torry Holt. The Titans responded with a field goal, but the Rams quickly extended their lead with another touchdown pass from Warner, this time to Isaac Bruce.

The Titans managed to score a touchdown just before halftime to cut the lead to 9-16, but the Rams continued to dominate in the second half. Warner threw another touchdown pass to Bruce, and running back Marshall Faulk added a rushing touchdown to put the game seemingly out of reach, with the Rams leading 23-6.

However, the Titans rallied late in the game, scoring two touchdowns in the fourth quarter to tie the game at 16-16 with just over two minutes remaining. The Rams had one more chance to win the game, and they took advantage, driving down the field and kicking a game-winning field goal as time expired.

The win was a historic moment for the Rams, who had never won a Super Bowl before. It was also a testament to the team's high-powered offense and the leadership of their quarterback, Kurt Warner, who was named the game's MVP.

Super Bowl XXXIV was an exciting and unforgettable game, featuring two teams that had overcome the odds to make it to the big game. The game showcased the importance of strong quarterback play and demonstrated how one play can make all the difference in a championship game. It remains one of the most memorable Super Bowls in NFL history.

In conclusion, the year 1999 was a significant one for the NFL. The expansion of the league, the on-field performances of standout players and teams, and the off-field issues that arose all contributed to a year that was filled with change and controversy. Looking back, it is clear that the events of 1999 set the stage for the growth and expansion that the NFL would experience in the years to come.

THE 2000'S

2000

The year 2000 was a landmark year for the NFL. The league was entering the new millennium and was poised for growth and expansion. The NFL had made significant changes in the previous year, including the addition of two new teams, and the league was ready to build on that momentum.

The Emergence of the New England Patriots

The 2000 season saw the emergence of the New England Patriots as a powerhouse in the NFL. Led by quarterback Tom Brady, who had taken over as the team's starter in the second game of the season, the Patriots finished with an 11-5 record and qualified for the playoffs as a wildcard team.

The Patriots' victory in the Super Bowl marked the beginning of a dynasty that would see the team win six Super Bowl championships in the next two decades. The team's success was a testament to the importance of strong leadership and strategic planning, as well as the value of having a franchise quarterback.

Expansion of the NFL

In 2000, the NFL continued its expansion with the addition of a 32nd team, the Houston Texans. The Texans joined the league as an expansion team and played their first game in September of that year. The addition of the Texans was seen as a significant milestone for the NFL, as it marked the first time in over 20 years that the league had added a new team.

The Texans were not the only expansion team to make news in 2000. The Cleveland Browns, who had returned to the NFL in 1999 after a three-year absence, unveiled their new uniforms and logo. The team's new look was met with mixed reviews, but it was seen as a positive step for a franchise that had been struggling for several years.

Off-Field Issues

Off-field issues continued to be a concern for the NFL in 2000. The issue of player safety remained a hot topic, with several high-profile injuries occurring during the season. The league also faced criticism for its handling of concussion-related issues, with some former players filing lawsuits against the league over the issue.

Another off-field issue that received attention in 2000 was the issue of player conduct. Several players were arrested for various offenses, including assault and driving under the influence. The league responded by implementing stricter policies and penalties for players who engaged in off-field misconduct.

Super Bowl XXXV

Super Bowl XXXV was the championship game of the 2000 NFL season, played on January 28, 2001, at Raymond James Stadium in Tampa, Florida. The game featured the Baltimore Ravens and the New York Giants, two teams that had emerged as dominant forces in their respective conferences.

The Ravens were known for their suffocating defense, which had allowed just 165 points during the regular season. The Giants, on the other hand, had a balanced offense and a defense that had allowed just 246 points.

The game got off to a slow start, with both teams struggling to score in the first quarter. However, the Ravens broke through early in the second quarter with a touchdown pass from quarterback Trent Dilfer to wide receiver Brandon Stokley. The Giants responded with a field goal, but the Ravens quickly extended their lead with another touchdown pass from Dilfer, this time to tight end Shannon Sharpe.

The Ravens continued to dominate in the second half, with their defense shutting down the Giants' offense. The Ravens added two more touchdowns in the third quarter, one on a touchdown pass from Dilfer to running back Jamal Lewis, and another on a 47-yard interception return by Duane Starks.

The Giants managed to score a touchdown in the fourth quarter, but it was too little, too late, as the Ravens held on for a 34-7 victory. The win was a historic moment for the Ravens, who had never won a Super Bowl before. It was also a testament to their dominant defense, which had allowed just 23 points in four playoff games.

Ray Lewis, the Ravens' star linebacker, was named the game's MVP for his performance, which included three tackles, four passes defended, and a crucial interception. Super Bowl XXXV was a showcase of the importance of defense in football, and the Ravens' victory demonstrated how a strong defense can carry a team to a championship.

The year 2000 was a significant year for the NFL. The emergence of the New England Patriots as a dominant force in the league, the expansion of the league with the addition of the Houston Texans, and the continued focus on off-field issues all contributed to a year that was filled with change and controversy. Looking back, it is clear that the events of 2000 set the stage for the growth and expansion that the NFL would experience in the years to come.

2001

The year 2001 was a year of great triumph and tragedy for the NFL. On the one hand, the league saw some of its greatest moments, with the emergence of new stars and the crowning of a new Super Bowl champion. On the other hand, the year was marked by a tragic event that would change the course of history and have a profound impact on the NFL and the world at large.

The Emergence of New Stars

In 2001, a number of young players emerged as stars in the NFL. One of the most notable was quarterback Michael Vick of the Atlanta Falcons. Vick, who was the first overall pick in the 2001 NFL Draft, quickly became known for his incredible athleticism and playmaking ability. He helped lead the Falcons to a playoff berth in his rookie season and became one of the league's most exciting players.

Another emerging star in 2001 was running back LaDainian Tomlinson of the San Diego Chargers. Tomlinson, who was drafted in the first round in 2001, had an incredible rookie season, rushing for over 1,200 yards and scoring 10 touchdowns. He would go on to have a Hall of Fame career, retiring as one of the greatest running backs in NFL history.

The Patriots Repeat

In 2001, the New England Patriots won their second Super Bowl championship in three years. Led by quarterback Tom Brady and a stout defense, the Patriots defeated the heavily favored St. Louis Rams in Super Bowl XXXVI.

The victory solidified the Patriots' status as one of the NFL's premier teams and cemented Brady's reputation as one of the league's best quarterbacks.

Super Bowl XXXVI

Super Bowl XXXVI was played on February 3, 2002, at the Louisiana Superdome in New Orleans, Louisiana. It was a matchup between the New England Patriots, representing the AFC, and the St. Louis Rams, representing the NFC.

The Rams were the defending Super Bowl champions and came into the game as heavy favorites. They were led by quarterback Kurt Warner, who had thrown for 4,830 yards and 36 touchdowns during the regular season. The Patriots, on the other hand, were led by second-year quarterback Tom Brady, who had taken over for an injured Drew Bledsoe during the regular season.

The game got off to a slow start, with both teams struggling to move the ball in the first quarter. However, the Patriots struck first in the second quarter with a field goal by kicker Adam Vinatieri. The Rams responded with a touchdown pass from Warner to wide receiver Ricky Proehl, taking a 7-3 lead into halftime.

In the second half, the Patriots' defense continued to stifle the Rams' high-powered offense. The Rams managed to tie the game with another touchdown pass from Warner to Proehl, but the Patriots answered back with a touchdown pass from Brady to wide receiver David Patten.

With just over a minute left in the game, the Rams had a chance to tie or win the game. However, their final drive was thwarted by an interception by Patriots' defensive back Ty Law, securing the victory for the Patriots.

The final score was 20-17 in favor of the Patriots, who had pulled off one of the biggest upsets in Super Bowl history. Tom Brady was named the game's MVP, completing 16 of 27 passes for 145 yards and a touchdown. The win marked the first Super Bowl victory for the Patriots franchise and the beginning of a dynasty, as they would go on to win five more Super Bowls over the next two decades.

Super Bowl XXXVI is remembered as one of the greatest upsets in Super Bowl history and a defining moment for Tom Brady and the New England Patriots. It was a thrilling game that showcased the importance of defense and the power of perseverance, as the underdog Patriots overcame the odds to win their first Super Bowl.

September 11th and Its Impact on the NFL

On September 11th, 2001, terrorists attacked the United States, killing thousands of people and causing widespread destruction. The attacks had a profound impact on the NFL, as well as on the entire country. The league canceled its games for the following weekend, and when play resumed the following week, there was a sense of unity and patriotism that permeated the league.

In the months that followed, the NFL implemented a number of new security measures to protect fans and players, including increased security screenings and restrictions on what could be brought into stadiums. The league also made a number of changes to its game-day experience, including the playing of the national anthem before each game.

The year 2001 was a year of great triumph and tragedy for the NFL. While the emergence of new stars and the Patriots' repeat as Super Bowl champions provided plenty of excitement, the terrorist attacks of September 11th cast a shadow over the year and forever changed the course of history. Despite the challenges, the NFL remained a symbol of strength and resilience, demonstrating the power of sports to bring people together in times of crisis.

2002

The year 2002 was a memorable one for the NFL. Many significant events took place, including the Super Bowl championship game, coaching changes, and player controversies.

Coaching Changes

The 2002 offseason saw several significant coaching changes, including Bill Parcells returning to the NFL to coach the Dallas Cowboys. He had previously retired from coaching after leading the New England Patriots to a Super Bowl victory in 1996.

Another notable change was Andy Reid taking over as the head coach of the Philadelphia Eagles. He led the team to four consecutive NFC Championship games from 2001 to 2004 and a Super Bowl appearance in 2005.

Player Controversies

Jovan Belcher and Rae Carruth were two NFL players involved in high-profile murder cases, which shocked the league and the wider public.

Jovan Belcher was a linebacker for the Kansas City Chiefs. In 2012, he killed his girlfriend, Kasandra Perkins, before driving to the team's training facility and taking his own life in front of his coach and general manager. The incident sparked widespread debate about gun control and mental health in the NFL. Belcher's actions were a tragic reminder of the toll that traumatic brain injuries and repeated hits to the head can have on players, as well as the importance of addressing mental health concerns in the league.

Rae Carruth was a wide receiver for the Carolina Panthers. In 1999, he hired a hitman to murder his pregnant girlfriend, Cherica Adams. Adams died a month later, but her child, Chancellor Lee Adams, survived and was born with cerebral palsy. Carruth was found guilty of conspiracy to commit murder and sentenced to 18-24 years in prison. The case garnered widespread media attention and highlighted the issue of domestic violence in the NFL.

Both cases demonstrated the need for the NFL to address issues related to mental health and domestic violence among its players. In response to these incidents and others like them, the NFL has implemented policies aimed at preventing domestic violence and supporting the mental health of its players. These policies include mandatory counseling for players involved in domestic violence incidents and increased resources for players struggling with mental health issues.

The cases of Jovan Belcher and Rae Carruth serve as tragic reminders of the importance of taking these issues seriously and addressing them proactively. While the NFL has made progress in addressing these problems, there is still much work to be done to ensure the safety and well-being of all players, both on and off the field.

Super Bowl XXXVII

Super Bowl XXXVII was played on January 26, 2003, at Qualcomm Stadium in San Diego, California. It was a matchup between the Tampa Bay Buccaneers, representing the NFC, and the Oakland Raiders, representing the AFC.

The Buccaneers were making their first-ever Super Bowl appearance, led by a ferocious defense that had allowed the fewest points in the league during the regular season. The Raiders, led by quarterback Rich Gannon, were seeking their fourth Super Bowl victory in franchise history.

The game got off to a fast start, with both teams trading touchdowns in the first quarter. However, it was the Buccaneers' defense that would take over the game. Tampa Bay's defense intercepted Gannon five times, returning three of those interceptions for touchdowns.

The Buccaneers' defense was led by safety Dexter Jackson, who intercepted two passes and was named the game's MVP. Linebacker Derrick Brooks also had a standout performance, returning an interception for a touchdown and leading the defense with six tackles.

On the offensive side of the ball, Buccaneers' quarterback Brad Johnson threw for 215 yards and two touchdowns, both to wide receiver Keenan McCardell. The Buccaneers' running game was also effective, with running back Michael Pittman rushing for 124 yards on 29 carries.

The Raiders managed to score another touchdown in the fourth quarter, but it was too little, too late. The final score was 48-21 in favor of the Buccaneers, who won their first-ever Super Bowl and became the first team in Super Bowl history to score three defensive touchdowns.

Super Bowl XXXVII is remembered as a dominant performance by the Tampa Bay Buccaneers' defense, which shut down one of the best offenses in the league and set a Super Bowl record with three defensive touchdowns. It was a defining moment for the Buccaneers' franchise, which had struggled for years before finally achieving their first Super Bowl victory.

The year 2002 was an eventful one for the NFL, with the Tampa Bay Buccaneers winning their first-ever Super Bowl championship, significant coaching changes, and player controversies. These events would have a lasting impact on the league and its players, coaches, and fans for years to come.

2003

The year 2003 was a significant year for the NFL. Many notable events took place, including the Super Bowl championship game, player milestones, and off-the-field controversies. This section will explore the most significant happenings in the league during that year.

Player Milestones

Emmitt Smith: In 2003, Emmitt Smith was still an active player in the NFL and was a member of the Arizona Cardinals. At this point in his career, Smith was no longer the dominant running back he had been earlier in his career, but he was still a productive player.

During the 2003 season, Smith rushed for 256 yards and two touchdowns in the first four games. However, he suffered a shoulder injury in Week 5 and was forced to miss the next three games. Despite the injury, Smith returned in Week 9 and continued to contribute to the Cardinals' offense.

On October 27, 2003, Smith made NFL history by becoming the league's all-time leading rusher. In a game against the Seattle Seahawks, Smith rushed for 109 yards on 24 carries, surpassing Walter Payton's previous record of 16,726 rushing yards. Smith's achievement was celebrated by fans and fellow players, and he was widely recognized as one of the greatest running backs of all time.

Smith continued to play for the Cardinals for two more seasons before retiring in 2005. He finished his career with 18,355 rushing yards and 164 rushing touchdowns, both of which remain NFL records to this day. Smith's accomplishments on the field cemented his legacy as one of the greatest players in NFL history.

Jerry Rice: In 2003, Jerry Rice was playing for the Oakland Raiders and was in his 19th season in the NFL. Despite his advanced age, Rice was still a productive player, and he was on the verge of setting a major NFL milestone.

On October 5, 2003, in a game against the Cleveland Browns, Rice caught his 1,102nd career reception, breaking the previous NFL record held by Cris Carter. The achievement was celebrated by Rice's teammates and coaches, as well as by NFL fans around the world.

Rice's record-setting reception was just one highlight of a long and illustrious career. Over his 20 seasons in the NFL, Rice set numerous records and established himself as one of the greatest wide receivers of all time. He finished his career with 1,549 receptions, 22,895 receiving yards, and 197 receiving touchdowns, all of which are still NFL records to this day.

Off-the-Field Controversies

The 2003 NFL season was not without its off-the-field controversies. One of the most significant was the case of Indianapolis Colts running back Ricky Williams, who was suspended for the entire season for violating the league's substance abuse policy. Williams would return to the NFL in 2004, but his career was never the same.

Super Bowl XXXVIII

Super Bowl XXXVIII was played on February 1, 2004, at Reliant Stadium in Houston, Texas. It was a matchup between the New England Patriots, representing the AFC, and the Carolina Panthers, representing the NFC.

The Patriots were led by quarterback Tom Brady, who was looking to win his second Super Bowl in three years. The Panthers, led by quarterback Jake Delhomme and a powerful rushing attack, were making their first Super Bowl appearance in franchise history.

The game was a closely contested battle from start to finish, with both teams trading touchdowns throughout the game. The Patriots got off to a quick start, with Brady throwing a touchdown pass to wide receiver Deion Branch on their first possession. However, the Panthers responded with two touchdowns of their own to take a 14-10 lead at halftime.

In the second half, the game continued to be a back-and-forth affair. The Patriots regained the lead in the third quarter on a touchdown pass from Brady to tight end Christian Fauria, but the Panthers responded with another touchdown to take a 22-21 lead.

With just over two minutes remaining in the game, the Patriots got the ball back and drove down the field. On the final drive, Brady completed several key passes to set up a 41-yard field goal attempt by kicker Adam Vinatieri. Vinatieri, who had famously kicked the game-winning field goal in Super Bowl XXXVI, drilled the kick through the uprights to give the Patriots a 32-29 lead.

The Panthers had one last chance to tie or win the game, but their final drive fell short. Delhomme's pass was intercepted by Patriots' safety Rodney Harrison with seconds remaining, sealing the victory for New England.

Brady was named the game's MVP, completing 32 of 48 passes for 354 yards and three touchdowns. Branch also had a standout performance, catching 10 passes for 143 yards and a touchdown.

Super Bowl XXXVIII is remembered as a thrilling, closely contested game between two talented teams. It was another defining moment for the Patriots' franchise, which had become one of the most dominant teams in the league under the leadership of Brady and head coach Bill Belichick.

Another controversial moment was the so-called "wardrobe malfunction" during the halftime show of Super Bowl XXXVIII. During a performance by Janet Jackson and Justin Timberlake, Jackson's breast was briefly exposed on live television. The incident sparked a nationwide controversy and led to increased scrutiny of television content.

The year 2003 was a memorable year for the NFL, with the New England Patriots winning their second Super Bowl championship in three years, player milestones, and off-the-field controversies. These events would have a lasting impact on the league and its players, coaches, and fans for years to come.

2004

The year 2004 was a significant year for the NFL. Many notable events took place, including the Super Bowl championship game, player milestones, and off-the-field controversies.

Player Milestones

The 2004 NFL season saw several player milestones. One of the most significant was Jerry Rice, who became the first player in NFL history to record 200 career touchdown receptions. Rice achieved this milestone on October 10, 2004, in a game against the New York Jets.

Another notable milestone was Curtis Martin, who became the oldest player in NFL history to win the league's rushing title. Martin rushed for 1,697 yards at the age of 31, becoming the first player over the age of 30 to lead the league in rushing since Walter Payton in 1985.

Super Bowl XXXIX

Super Bowl 39, also known as Super Bowl XXXIX, was held on February 6, 2005, at the Alltel Stadium in Jacksonville, Florida. The game featured the American Football Conference (AFC) champion New England Patriots and the National Football Conference (NFC) champion Philadelphia Eagles. It was the second Super Bowl matchup between these two teams, with the Patriots having won Super Bowl XXXIX four years earlier.

The game was highly anticipated, with both teams coming into the contest with impressive regular season records. The Patriots finished the season with a 14-2 record and were led by quarterback Tom Brady, who had already won two Super Bowl MVP awards. The Eagles, on the other hand, had a 13-3 record and were led by quarterback Donovan McNabb.

The first quarter of the game was a defensive battle, with neither team able to score. The Patriots got on the board early in the second quarter with a touchdown pass from Brady to wide receiver Deion Branch. The Eagles responded with a touchdown of their own, a 30-yard pass from McNabb to wide receiver Greg Lewis. However, the Patriots regained the lead with a touchdown pass from Brady to running back Kevin Faulk just before halftime, giving them a 14-7 lead.

The second half of the game was dominated by the Patriots, who scored another touchdown in the third quarter with a 2-yard run by running back Corey Dillon. The Eagles tried to mount a comeback in the fourth quarter, with McNabb connecting on a touchdown pass to tight end L.J. Smith, but it was not enough. The Patriots held on to win the game by a score of 24-21, becoming the first team since the 1998-1999 Denver Broncos to win consecutive Super Bowls.

Tom Brady was named the Super Bowl MVP for the third time in his career, completing 23 of 33 passes for 236 yards and two touchdowns. He also set a Super Bowl record with 16 consecutive completions during the game. The Patriots' defense was also instrumental in the victory, intercepting McNabb three times and sacking him four times.

Overall, Super Bowl XXXIX was a highly competitive game between two talented teams. The Patriots' victory cemented their status as one of the best teams in NFL history, while the Eagles' performance showed that they were a formidable opponent. The game was watched by an estimated 133.7 million viewers, making it one of the most-watched television events in history.

The year 2004 was a memorable year for the NFL, with the New England Patriots winning their third Super Bowl championship in four years, and player milestones. These events would have a lasting impact on the league and its players, coaches, and fans for years to come.

2005

The NFL is the premier professional American football league in the world. Founded in 1920, the NFL has grown into a massive business enterprise that generates billions of dollars in revenue each year. In 2005, the NFL was in the midst of a period of stability and growth, with new rules and innovations making the game more exciting than ever before.

The Teams

In 2005, the NFL featured 32 teams, divided into two conferences – the National Football Conference (NFC) and the American Football Conference (AFC) – with 16 teams in each conference. Each conference was further divided into four divisions, with four teams in each division.

The AFC consisted of the East, North, South, and West divisions, while the NFC was divided into the East, North, South, and West divisions. Some of the most popular teams in the league in 2005 included the New England Patriots, Indianapolis Colts, Pittsburgh Steelers, Philadelphia Eagles, and Dallas Cowboys.

The Players

The NFL is known for its incredible athletes, and 2005 was no exception. Some of the most famous players in the league in 2005 included quarterback Peyton Manning of the Indianapolis Colts, running back LaDainian Tomlinson of the San Diego Chargers, and wide receiver Terrell Owens of the Philadelphia Eagles.

Other notable players in the league at the time included quarterbacks Tom Brady of the New England Patriots and Donovan McNabb of the Philadelphia Eagles, running back Shaun Alexander of the Seattle Seahawks, and wide receivers Marvin Harrison of the Indianapolis Colts and Randy Moss of the Oakland Raiders.

The Rules

The NFL has always been known for its complex rules and regulations, and 2005 was no different. One of the biggest rule changes in 2005 was the implementation of the "horse-collar" rule, which prohibited players from tackling ball carriers by grabbing the back of their jerseys.

Other rule changes included stricter enforcement of defensive holding and illegal contact penalties, as well as an emphasis on player safety that led to increased fines and suspensions for players who engaged in dangerous or unsportsmanlike conduct.

The Games

The 2005 NFL season was filled with memorable games and moments. One of the most famous games of the season was Super Bowl XL, which was played on February 5, 2006, and featured the Pittsburgh Steelers and Seattle Seahawks. The Steelers won the game 21-10, with quarterback Ben Roethlisberger throwing for 123 yards and two touchdowns.

Other memorable games from the 2005 season included the "Music City Miracle II," in which the Tennessee Titans beat the Arizona Cardinals with a last-second touchdown pass, and the "Monday Night Miracle," in which the New York Giants came back from a 21-point deficit to beat the Dallas Cowboys in overtime.

The Business

The NFL is big business, and in 2005, the league continued to grow and expand its reach. The league's television ratings remained strong, with many of the most-watched programs on television being NFL games.

The league also continued to explore new revenue streams, including international expansion and new media ventures. In 2005, the league launched NFL Network, a 24-hour cable network that featured news, analysis, and live games.

Super Bowl XL

Super Bowl XL, also known as Super Bowl 40, was the championship game of the 2005 National Football League (NFL) season. It was played on February 5, 2006, at Ford Field in Detroit, Michigan. The Pittsburgh Steelers, representing the American Football Conference (AFC), faced off against the Seattle Seahawks, representing the National Football Conference (NFC), in what was expected to be an exciting and closely contested game.

The Steelers were led by their veteran quarterback, Ben Roethlisberger, who had already established himself as one of the league's top signal-callers despite being in just his second season. Roethlisberger was supported by a strong running game featuring running back Jerome Bettis, as well as a stingy defense that had allowed the fewest yards in the league during the regular season.

The Seahawks, meanwhile, were led by quarterback Matt Hasselbeck, who had thrown for over 3,000 yards during the regular season. The team also boasted a strong running game, with Shaun Alexander leading the league in rushing yards and touchdowns.

The game got off to a slow start, with both teams trading punts on their first few possessions. However, the Steelers struck first midway through the first quarter, with Roethlisberger hitting wide receiver Antwaan Randle El for a 43-yard touchdown pass.

Seattle answered back with a field goal early in the second quarter, but the Steelers added to their lead with a pair of field goals of their own to go up 13-3 at halftime.

In the third quarter, the Seahawks appeared to be gaining momentum, driving deep into Steelers territory. However, Hasselbeck threw an interception to Pittsburgh's Ike Taylor, who returned it 24 yards to set up a Bettis touchdown run that put the Steelers up 20-3.

Seattle continued to fight back, with Hasselbeck connecting with wide receiver Darrell Jackson for a touchdown to cut the lead to 20-10. However, the Steelers responded with another touchdown run from Bettis, who was playing in what would be his final game before retiring. Seattle added a late touchdown, but it was too little, too late, as the Steelers held on for a 21-10 victory.

Roethlisberger was named the game's Most Valuable Player, completing 9 of 21 passes for 123 yards and a touchdown. Bettis finished with 43 yards rushing and two touchdowns, while the Steelers defense held the Seahawks to just 3 points through the first three quarters.

Super Bowl XL was not without controversy, however. Referee Bill Leavy's crew was criticized for several questionable calls, including a holding penalty that nullified a touchdown for Seattle and a pass interference call against the Seahawks that led to a Pittsburgh touchdown.

Nevertheless, the Steelers emerged victorious, claiming their fifth Super Bowl championship in franchise history.

The NFL in 2005 was a league in transition, with new rules and innovations making the game more exciting and player safety becoming a top priority. The league continued to grow and expand its reach, with new revenue streams and international expansion on the horizon. As the NFL continued to evolve, fans looked forward to many more exciting seasons to come.

2006

The year 2006 was an eventful year for the NFL, marked by exciting games, memorable performances, and important changes in the league's rules and policies.

The Teams

In 2006, the NFL featured 32 teams, divided into two conferences – the National Football Conference (NFC) and the American Football Conference (AFC) – with 16 teams in each conference. Each conference was further divided into four divisions, with four teams in each division.

Some of the most popular teams in the league in 2006 included the Indianapolis Colts, New Orleans Saints, Chicago Bears, San Diego Chargers, and New England Patriots.

The Players

The NFL is known for its incredible athletes, and 2006 was no exception. Some of the most famous players in the league in 2006 included quarterback Peyton Manning of the Indianapolis Colts, running back LaDainian Tomlinson of the San Diego Chargers, and wide receiver Chad Johnson of the Cincinnati Bengals.

Other notable players in the league at the time included quarterbacks Tom Brady of the New England Patriots and Drew Brees of the New Orleans Saints, running back Shaun Alexander of the Seattle Seahawks, and wide receivers Steve Smith of the Carolina Panthers and Terrell Owens of the Dallas Cowboys.

The Rules

The NFL is constantly refining its rules and regulations, and 2006 saw several changes to the game. One of the biggest rule changes in 2006 was the introduction of the "roughing the passer" penalty, which prohibited defenders from hitting quarterbacks in the head or below the knees.

Other rule changes included stricter enforcement of unsportsmanlike conduct penalties, as well as an emphasis on player safety that led to increased fines and suspensions for players who engaged in dangerous or violent conduct on the field.

The Games

The 2006 NFL season was filled with memorable games and moments. One of the most famous games of the season was the NFC Championship Game between the New Orleans Saints and the Chicago Bears, which featured a controversial decision by Saints head coach Sean Payton to attempt an onside kick early in the game.

Other memorable games from the 2006 season included the "Miracle at the Meadowlands," in which the New York Giants beat the Philadelphia Eagles with a last-second touchdown pass, and the "Monday Night Massacre," in which the Chicago Bears beat the Arizona Cardinals 24-23 after scoring three touchdowns in the final quarter.

The Business

The NFL continued to be a highly profitable enterprise in 2006, with strong television ratings and robust revenue streams. The league also continued to explore new business opportunities, including international expansion and new media ventures.

In 2006, the NFL signed a landmark deal with NBC to broadcast Sunday Night Football, a new prime-time game that quickly became one of the most-watched programs on television.

Super Bowl XLI

Super Bowl XLI was the championship game of the 2006 National Football League (NFL) season, played on February 4, 2007, at Dolphin Stadium in Miami Gardens, Florida. The Indianapolis Colts, representing the American Football Conference (AFC), faced off against the Chicago Bears, representing the National Football Conference (NFC), in a highly anticipated matchup.

The Colts were led by quarterback Peyton Manning, who had established himself as one of the greatest quarterbacks in NFL history. Manning had thrown for over 4,000 yards during the regular season and led the Colts to a 12-4 record. He was supported by a strong running game, featuring running backs Joseph Addai and Dominic Rhodes, as well as a solid defense.

The Bears, meanwhile, were led by a dominant defense that had allowed the fewest points in the league during the regular season. The offense was led by quarterback Rex Grossman, who had thrown for over 3,000 yards but had struggled with inconsistency throughout the season.

The game got off to a slow start, with both teams struggling to move the ball early on. The Colts struck first with a field goal midway through the first quarter, but the Bears answered back with a touchdown run by running back Thomas Jones to take a 7-3 lead.

In the second quarter, the Colts took control of the game, with Manning connecting with wide receiver Reggie Wayne for a touchdown and then finding tight end Dallas Clark for another score. The Bears added a field goal before halftime, but the Colts led 16-7 at the break.

The third quarter saw more of the same, with the Colts extending their lead with another field goal before the Bears added a touchdown run by Grossman to cut the lead to 19-14. However, the Colts pulled away in the fourth quarter, with Addai scoring a touchdown run and then Manning finding Wayne for another score to put the game out of reach.

Manning was named the game's Most Valuable Player, completing 25 of 38 passes for 247 yards and a touchdown. Addai finished with 77 yards rushing and a touchdown, while Wayne had 10 catches for 100 yards and a score.

Super Bowl XLI was also notable for being played in the rain, which made for a challenging playing surface for both teams. Despite the conditions, the Colts were able to execute their game plan and come away with the victory, claiming their first Super Bowl championship since moving to Indianapolis in 1984.

The game marked a significant milestone for Manning, who had finally won a Super Bowl after years of playoff disappointments. It also solidified his legacy as one of the greatest quarterbacks in NFL history, and helped to cement the Colts' place among the league's elite teams.

The NFL in 2006 was a league in transition, with new rules and innovations making the game safer and more exciting for fans. The league continued to grow and expand its reach, with new revenue streams and international expansion on the horizon. As the NFL continued to evolve, fans looked forward to many more exciting seasons to come.

2007

The NFL is a premier professional American football league in the world. The year 2007 was an exciting year for the NFL, marked by thrilling games, impressive performances, and important changes in the league's landscape.

The Teams

In 2007, the NFL featured 32 teams, divided into two conferences – the National Football Conference (NFC) and the American Football Conference (AFC) – with 16 teams in each conference. Each conference was further divided into four divisions, with four teams in each division.

Some of the most popular teams in the league in 2007 included the New England Patriots, Dallas Cowboys, Green Bay Packers, Indianapolis Colts, and New York Giants.

The Players

The NFL is known for its exceptional athletes, and 2007 was no exception. Some of the most famous players in the league in 2007 included quarterback Tom Brady of the New England Patriots, running back Adrian Peterson of the Minnesota Vikings, and wide receiver Randy Moss of the New England Patriots.

Other notable players in the league at the time included quarterbacks Peyton Manning of the Indianapolis Colts and Tony Romo of the Dallas Cowboys, running back LaDainian Tomlinson of the San Diego Chargers, and wide receivers Terrell Owens of the Dallas Cowboys and T.J. Houshmandzadeh of the Cincinnati Bengals.

The Rules

The NFL is always looking to improve the game, and 2007 saw several rule changes. One of the most significant rule changes in 2007 was the implementation of a stricter policy on player conduct, including fines and suspensions for players who violated league policies.

Other rule changes included a modification to the instant replay system, allowing coaches to challenge up to two calls per game, and the removal of the "force-out" rule, which had previously allowed receivers to catch the ball while being pushed out of bounds.

The Games

The 2007 NFL season was filled with memorable games and moments

Super Bowl XLII

Super Bowl XLII was played on February 3, 2008, at the University of Phoenix Stadium in Glendale, Arizona. The game featured the New York Giants, the NFC champions, and the New England Patriots, the AFC champions.

The Patriots entered the game as heavy favorites, having completed an undefeated regular season and two playoff victories en route to their fifth Super Bowl appearance in seven years. The Giants, on the other hand, had finished the regular season with a 10-6 record and had to win three road playoff games to reach the Super Bowl.

The game was a defensive battle from the start, with both teams struggling to move the ball and score points. The Patriots took a 7-3 lead early in the second quarter, but the Giants responded with a field goal to cut the deficit to 7-6 at halftime.

In the second half, the Giants defense continued to pressure Patriots quarterback Tom Brady, sacking him five times and forcing him into several costly mistakes. The Giants took their first lead of the game midway through the fourth quarter, with a touchdown pass from quarterback Eli Manning to receiver David Tyree on a miraculous play that has become known as the "Helmet Catch."

The Patriots had a chance to tie the game on their final drive, but a last-second hail mary pass fell incomplete, securing a 17-14 victory for the Giants. Manning was named the game's MVP after completing 19 of 34 passes for 255 yards and two touchdowns.

The Giants' victory over the previously unbeaten Patriots in Super Bowl XLII is widely considered one of the greatest upsets in NFL history and remains a cherished memory for Giants fans to this day.

Other memorable games from the 2007 season included the "Monday Night Meltdown," in which the Dallas Cowboys came back from a 24-point deficit to defeat the Buffalo Bills, and the "Snow Bowl," in which the Green Bay Packers beat the Seattle Seahawks in a snowstorm.

The Business

The NFL continued to be a highly profitable enterprise in 2007, with strong television ratings and robust revenue streams. The league also continued to explore new business opportunities, including international expansion and new media ventures.

In 2007, the NFL signed a new collective bargaining agreement with the NFL Players Association, ensuring labor peace and stability for the league and its players.

The NFL in 2007 was a league in transition, with new rules and innovations making the game safer and more exciting for fans. The league continued to grow and expand its reach, with new revenue streams and international expansion on the horizon. As the NFL continued to evolve, fans looked forward to many more exciting seasons to come.

2008

The year 2008 marked the 89th season of the NFL, the premier professional American football league in the world. The 2008 NFL season was filled with thrilling games, outstanding performances, and important changes in the league's landscape.

The Teams

In 2008, the NFL featured 32 teams, divided into two conferences – the National Football Conference (NFC) and the American Football Conference (AFC) – with 16 teams in each conference. Each conference was further divided into four divisions, with four teams in each division.

Some of the most popular teams in the league in 2008 included the Pittsburgh Steelers, New York Giants, Dallas Cowboys, Indianapolis Colts, and New England Patriots.

The Players

The NFL is known for its exceptional athletes, and 2008 was no exception. Some of the most famous players in the league in 2008 included quarterbacks Peyton Manning of the Indianapolis Colts, Tom Brady of the New England Patriots, and Brett Favre of the New York Jets.

Other notable players in the league at the time included running backs Adrian Peterson of the Minnesota Vikings and Michael Turner of the Atlanta Falcons, and wide receivers Larry Fitzgerald of the Arizona Cardinals and Andre Johnson of the Houston Texans.

The Rules

The NFL is always looking to improve the game, and 2008 saw several rule changes. One of the most significant rule changes in 2008 was the implementation of the "force-out" rule, which had previously been removed in 2007.

Other rule changes included the prohibition of players using their helmets as weapons, an increase in the size of practice squads from 8 to 10 players, and the adoption of a new instant replay system that allowed coaches to challenge any call except scoring plays, which were subject to booth reviews.

Super Bowl XLIII

Super Bowl XLIII was the championship game of the 2008 NFL season and was played on February 1, 2009, at Raymond James Stadium in Tampa, Florida. The game featured the Pittsburgh Steelers, the AFC champions, and the Arizona Cardinals, the NFC champions.

The game was a back-and-forth affair, with both teams trading touchdowns throughout the first three quarters. The Steelers took a 20-7 lead early in the fourth quarter, but the Cardinals responded with two quick touchdowns to take a 23-20 lead with just over two minutes left in the game.

The Steelers then mounted a dramatic drive, highlighted by a 40-yard reception by Santonio Holmes, which put them on the Cardinals' six-yard line with just 35 seconds left in the game. On the next play, quarterback Ben Roethlisberger found Holmes in the back of the end zone for the game-winning touchdown, giving the Steelers a 27-23 victory.

Holmes was named the game's MVP after catching nine passes for 131 yards and the game-winning touchdown. Roethlisberger finished the game with 256 passing yards and one touchdown.

The victory was the sixth Super Bowl championship for the Steelers, tying them with the Dallas Cowboys for the most in NFL history. The game was also notable for being the first Super Bowl played between two teams that had never played each other in the regular season.

Other memorable games from the 2008 season included the "Monday Night Miracle," in which the Miami Dolphins came back from a 21-point deficit to beat the New York Jets, and the "Helmet Catch II," in which Eli Manning and the New York Giants defeated the Pittsburgh Steelers in a rematch of the previous year's Super Bowl.

The Business

The NFL continued to be a highly profitable enterprise in 2008, with strong television ratings and robust revenue streams. The league also continued to explore new business opportunities, including international expansion and new media ventures.

In 2008, the NFL also announced plans to build a new stadium for the Dallas Cowboys, which would become the largest domed stadium in the world when it opened in 2009.

The NFL in 2008 was a league in transition, with new rules and innovations making the game safer and more exciting for fans. The league continued to grow and expand its reach, with new revenue streams and international expansion on the horizon. As the NFL continued to evolve, fans looked forward to many more exciting seasons to come.

2009

The 2009 season marked the 90th season of the NFL, the premier professional American football league in the world. The 2009 season was filled with exciting games, standout performances, and significant changes in the league's landscape.

The Teams

In 2009, the NFL featured 32 teams, divided into two conferences – the National Football Conference (NFC) and the American Football Conference (AFC) – with 16 teams in each conference. Each conference was further divided into four divisions, with four teams in each division.

Some of the most popular teams in the league in 2009 included the Indianapolis Colts, New Orleans Saints, Minnesota Vikings, New England Patriots, and Pittsburgh Steelers.

The Players

The NFL is known for its exceptional athletes, and 2009 was no exception. Some of the most famous players in the league in 2009 included quarterbacks Peyton Manning of the Indianapolis Colts, Tom Brady of the New England Patriots, and Drew Brees of the New Orleans Saints.

Other notable players in the league at the time included running backs Chris Johnson of the Tennessee Titans and Adrian Peterson of the Minnesota Vikings, and wide receivers Andre Johnson of the Houston Texans and Larry Fitzgerald of the Arizona Cardinals.

The Rules

The NFL is always looking to improve the game, and 2009 saw several rule changes. One of the most significant rule changes in 2009 was the implementation of the "five-yard face mask" penalty, which made it illegal for a defender to grab and twist the face mask of an opponent.

Other rule changes included the expansion of the "horse-collar" rule to protect quarterbacks and kickers, and the elimination of the "force-out" rule that had been re-implemented the previous year.

The Games

The 2009 NFL season was filled with memorable games and moments. One of the most famous games of the season was the NFC Championship Game between the Minnesota

Vikings and New Orleans Saints, which featured a dramatic overtime finish and a game-winning field goal by Saints kicker Garrett Hartley.

Other memorable games from the 2009 season included the Indianapolis Colts' comeback victory over the New England Patriots in Week 10, and the "MNF Miracle," in which the Miami Dolphins scored two touchdowns in the final 2:01 to defeat the New York Jets.

Super Bowl XLIV

Super Bowl XLIV was the championship game of the 2009 NFL season and was played on February 7, 2010, at Sun Life Stadium in Miami Gardens, Florida. The game featured the AFC champions, the Indianapolis Colts, and the NFC champions, the New Orleans Saints.

The game was a closely contested matchup, with both teams trading touchdowns throughout the first three quarters. The Colts took a 10-0 lead in the first quarter, but the Saints responded with a touchdown in the second quarter to make it 10-7 at halftime.

In the second half, the game remained close, with the Colts leading 17-16 going into the fourth quarter. However, the Saints took the lead early in the fourth quarter with a touchdown pass from quarterback Drew Brees to Jeremy Shockey, and they extended their lead with a field goal later in the quarter.

The Colts had a chance to tie the game in the final minutes, but a interception by Saints cornerback Tracy Porter sealed the victory for New Orleans, with the final score of 31-17.

Drew Brees was named the game's MVP after completing 32 of 39 passes for 288 yards and two touchdowns. The victory was the first Super Bowl championship in Saints history, and it came in a season that was emotionally charged for the city of New Orleans, which was still recovering from Hurricane Katrina.

The game was also notable for featuring the first onside kick attempt in a Super Bowl during the second half, which the Saints successfully recovered and eventually led to a touchdown, and for being the first Super Bowl played in Miami in 10 years.

The Business

The NFL continued to be a highly profitable enterprise in 2009, with strong television ratings and robust revenue streams. The league also continued to explore new business opportunities, including international expansion and new media ventures.

In 2009, the NFL announced plans to play regular-season games in London for the third consecutive year, further expanding its reach beyond North America.

The NFL in 2009 was a league in transition, with new rules and innovations making the game safer and more exciting for fans. The league continued to grow and expand its reach, with new revenue streams and international expansion on the horizon. As the NFL continued to evolve, fans looked forward to many more exciting seasons to come.

THE 2010'S

2010

The NFL in the year 2010 was marked by several significant events, including rule changes, player retirements, and notable performances on the field.

Rule Changes

The NFL implemented several rule changes for the 2010 season, including changes to the enforcement of helmet-to-helmet hits, the definition of a catch, and the kickoff rules. The new kickoff rule required that kicking teams start from the 35-yard line instead of the 30-yard line, with the goal of reducing the number of high-speed collisions on kickoffs.

Player Retirements

Several prominent players retired after the 2009 season, including quarterback Brett Favre, who retired from the Minnesota Vikings after a long and successful career. Other notable retirees included running back LaDainian Tomlinson, who retired after 11 seasons with the San Diego Chargers and New York Jets, and wide receiver Torry Holt, who retired after 11 seasons with the St. Louis Rams and Jacksonville Jaguars.

On-Field Performances

Several players had outstanding performances during the 2010 season, including quarterbacks Tom Brady, Aaron Rodgers, and Drew Brees. Brady led the New England Patriots to a 14-2 record and threw for 36 touchdowns, earning him the league's MVP award. Rodgers led the Green Bay Packers to a Super Bowl championship, throwing for 304 yards and three touchdowns in the Super

Bowl, earning him the game's MVP award. Brees led the New Orleans Saints to a 11-5 record and threw for 33 touchdowns, earning him a Pro Bowl selection.

Other notable performances included running back Arian Foster, who rushed for 1,616 yards and 16 touchdowns for the Houston Texans, and wide receiver Calvin Johnson, who caught 77 passes for 1,120 yards and 12 touchdowns for the Detroit Lions.

Super Bowl XLV

The 2010 NFL season culminated in Super Bowl XLV, which was played on February 6, 2011, at Cowboys Stadium in Arlington, Texas. The game featured the AFC champions, the Pittsburgh Steelers, and the NFC champions, the Green Bay Packers.

The Packers took an early lead in the game and never trailed, holding off a late comeback attempt by the Steelers to win the game 31-25. Aaron Rodgers was named the game's MVP after throwing for 304 yards and three touchdowns.

The victory was the Packers' fourth Super Bowl championship in team history and marked the end of a remarkable postseason run in which they won three straight road games to reach the Super Bowl. The game was watched by an estimated 111 million viewers, making it the most-watched television program in U.S. history at the time.

Overall, the 2010 NFL season provided fans with exciting games, memorable moments, and plenty of drama. It set the stage for future seasons and helped to solidify the NFL's status as one of the most popular and beloved sports leagues in the world.

2011

The NFL in the year 2011 was marked by several significant events, including a lockout, rule changes, and notable performances on the field.

Lockout

The NFL experienced a lockout in 2011, which lasted from March 12 to July 25. The lockout was caused by a dispute between team owners and players over revenue sharing and other issues. The lockout threatened to delay or cancel the 2011 season, but an agreement was reached in July, and the season began on time.

Rule Changes

The NFL implemented several rule changes for the 2011 season, including changes to the enforcement of player safety rules, the definition of a catch, and the review process for scoring plays. The new player safety rules were designed to reduce the number of head and neck injuries, and included stricter penalties for helmet-to-helmet hits.

On-Field Performances

Several players had outstanding performances during the 2011 season, including quarterbacks Aaron Rodgers, Drew Brees, and Tom Brady. Rodgers led the Green Bay Packers to a 15-1 record and threw for 45 touchdowns, earning him the league's MVP award. Brees led the New Orleans Saints to a 13-3 record and threw for 5,476 yards and 46 touchdowns, breaking Dan Marino's single-season record for passing yards. Brady led the New England Patriots to a 13-3 record and threw for 5,235 yards and 39 touchdowns, earning him a Pro Bowl selection.

Other notable performances included running back LeSean McCoy, who rushed for 1,309 yards and 17 touchdowns for the Philadelphia Eagles, and wide receiver Calvin Johnson, who caught 96 passes for 1,681 yards and 16 touchdowns for the Detroit Lions.

Super Bowl XLVI

The 2011 NFL season culminated in Super Bowl XLVI, which was played on February 5, 2012, at Lucas Oil Stadium in Indianapolis, Indiana. The game featured the AFC champions, the New England Patriots, and the NFC champions, the New York Giants.

The game was closely contested throughout, with the Giants taking an early lead and the Patriots tying the game late in the fourth quarter. However, the Giants drove down the field and scored a game-winning touchdown with just under a minute remaining, winning the game 21-17. Giants quarterback Eli Manning was named the game's MVP after throwing for 296 yards and one touchdown.

The victory was the Giants' fourth Super Bowl championship in team history and marked the end of an exciting season that saw several teams emerge as contenders. The game was watched by an estimated 111.3 million viewers, making it the second-most-watched television program in U.S. history at the time.

The 2011 NFL season was a memorable one, with several notable events and performances on and off the field. The lockout threatened to delay or cancel the season, but an agreement was reached, and the season began on time. The season was marked by rule changes designed to promote player safety, and several players had outstanding performances, including Aaron Rodgers, Drew Brees, and Tom Brady. The season culminated in Super Bowl XLVI, which was won by the New York Giants, capping off an exciting and memorable year for the NFL.

2012

The 2012 NFL season was filled with drama, excitement, and a number of historic moments. From record-breaking performances to unexpected upsets, here are some of the highlights of the year.

On-Field Performances

Several players had standout performances during the 2012 season, including quarterbacks Peyton Manning and Tom Brady, who both threw for over 4,800 yards and 30 touchdowns. Manning, who was playing his first season with the Denver Broncos, earned his fifth NFL MVP award after throwing for 4,659 yards and 37 touchdowns.

Other notable performances included running back Adrian Peterson, who rushed for 2,097 yards and 12 touchdowns for the Minnesota Vikings, and wide receiver Calvin Johnson, who caught 122 passes for 1,964 yards and 5 touchdowns for the Detroit Lions, breaking Jerry Rice's single-season record for receiving yards.

Record-Breaking Moments

During the 2012 NFL season, there were several record-breaking moments that stood out:

1. Drew Brees breaks Johnny Unitas' record: In a game against the San Diego Chargers, New Orleans Saints quarterback Drew Brees broke Johnny Unitas' record for consecutive games with a touchdown pass, which had stood for 52 years. Brees went on to extend the record to 54 games.

2. Adrian Peterson rushes for over 2,000 yards: Minnesota Vikings running back Adrian Peterson had an incredible season, rushing for 2,097 yards, which is the second-highest single-season total in NFL history. He also came just nine yards short of breaking Eric Dickerson's record of 2,105 yards.

3. Calvin Johnson breaks Jerry Rice's receiving record: Detroit Lions wide receiver Calvin Johnson broke Jerry Rice's single-season record for receiving yards with 1,964. Johnson surpassed Rice's mark of 1,848 yards, which had stood for 17 years.

4. Peyton Manning's comeback season: After missing the entire 2011 season due to injury, Denver Broncos quarterback Peyton Manning had a record-breaking season in 2012. He set a new franchise record for passing yards in a single season with 4,659 and tied the NFL record for most games with three or more touchdown passes in a season with nine.

Overall, the 2012 NFL season was full of impressive performances and record-breaking moments from some of the league's greatest players.

Off-Field Controversies

The 2012 season was also marked by several off-field controversies, including the New Orleans Saints' "Bountygate" scandal, in which the team was found to have paid players for injuring opponents. As a result of the scandal, several Saints coaches and players were suspended, and the team was fined and lost draft picks.

Super Bowl XLVII

Super Bowl XLVII was played on February 3, 2013, at the Mercedes-Benz Superdome in New Orleans, Louisiana. The game featured the Baltimore Ravens, representing the American Football Conference (AFC), and the San Francisco 49ers, representing the National Football Conference (NFC). This Super Bowl would become one of the most memorable in NFL history, not just for the thrilling game on the field but also for the dramatic circumstances surrounding the game.

The game started off with a bang, as the Ravens scored on their first drive of the game with a touchdown pass from quarterback Joe Flacco to wide receiver Anquan Boldin. The 49ers struggled in the first half, with quarterback Colin Kaepernick throwing an interception that was returned for a touchdown by Ravens' cornerback Ed Reed. The Ravens took a commanding 21-6 lead into halftime, but the game was far from over.

The 49ers mounted a comeback in the third quarter, with Kaepernick connecting with tight end Vernon Davis for a touchdown to cut the lead to 21-13. After a Ravens field goal, Kaepernick scored on a 15-yard touchdown run to bring the 49ers within two points. However, a failed two-point conversion left the score at 28-26 in favor of the Ravens.

The fourth quarter was full of drama and excitement. With just over 10 minutes remaining in the game, a power outage caused a 34-minute delay in the action, leading to an unprecedented break in Super Bowl history. When play resumed, the 49ers continued their comeback effort, scoring a field goal to cut the lead to 28-23.

With just over two minutes remaining, the 49ers drove down the field and had a chance to take the lead, but were stopped just short of the goal line on a controversial non-call for pass interference. The Ravens held on and took over on downs, but were backed up near their own end zone.

On the ensuing play, Ravens' punter Sam Koch ran out of the back of the end zone for a safety, cutting the Ravens' lead to 34-31. The 49ers had one last chance to win the game, but the Ravens defense held strong, stopping the 49ers on a fourth-down play to seal the victory.

Joe Flacco was named the game's Most Valuable Player, completing 22 of 33 passes for 287 yards and three touchdowns. The Ravens' defense also played a key role in the victory, intercepting Kaepernick twice and holding the 49ers to just 6 points in the first half.

Super Bowl XLVII will be remembered not just for the thrilling game on the field, but also for the dramatic circumstances surrounding the game, including the power outage and controversial non-call. It will go down as one of the most memorable Super Bowls in NFL history, and cemented the Ravens as one of the league's most successful franchises.

The 2012 NFL season was an exciting one, filled with record-breaking performances, unexpected upsets, and off-field controversies. Several players had standout seasons, including Peyton Manning, Adrian Peterson, and Calvin Johnson, and the season culminated in a thrilling Super Bowl matchup between the Baltimore Ravens and the San Francisco 49ers. Despite the challenges and controversies of the year, the NFL continued to be one of the most popular and beloved sports leagues in the world, and the 2012 season will be remembered as another chapter in the league's rich history.

2013

The NFL in the year 2013 was marked by exciting games, intense rivalries, and high-stakes playoffs. The league was dominated by teams like the Seattle Seahawks, Denver Broncos, and San Francisco 49ers, which showcased some of the most talented players in the game.

The Season

The 2013 NFL season kicked off on September 5th with a matchup between the Denver Broncos and the Baltimore Ravens. The game was a rematch of the previous year's AFC Divisional playoff game, in which the Ravens upset the Broncos in double-overtime. However, this time, the Broncos dominated the game, winning 49-27.

Throughout the season, several teams emerged as top contenders for the Super Bowl. The Seattle Seahawks, led by quarterback Russell Wilson, had the best record in the league at 13-3. The Denver Broncos, led by quarterback Peyton Manning, set numerous offensive records and finished with a 13-3 record as well. The San Francisco 49ers, led by quarterback Colin Kaepernick, finished with a 12-4 record.

The playoffs were marked by several exciting matchups. The San Francisco 49ers defeated the Green Bay Packers in the Wild Card round, followed by a dramatic victory over the Carolina Panthers in the Divisional round. The Seattle Seahawks dominated the New Orleans Saints in the Divisional round, while the Denver Broncos defeated the San Diego Chargers.

The Conference Championships were a showdown between the top teams in each conference. The Denver Broncos faced off against the New England Patriots in the AFC

Championship game, while the Seattle Seahawks took on the San Francisco 49ers in the NFC Championship game. The Broncos defeated the Patriots 26-16 to advance to the Super Bowl, while the Seahawks edged out the 49ers 23-17 in a dramatic finish.

Players

Several players had outstanding performances during the 2013 NFL season. Denver Broncos quarterback Peyton Manning set a new NFL record for most touchdown passes in a single season, with 55. Seattle Seahawks cornerback Richard Sherman was named the league's Defensive Player of the Year, while his teammate, running back Marshawn Lynch, rushed for over 1,200 yards and 12 touchdowns.

Other notable players from the 2013 season include New Orleans Saints quarterback Drew Brees, who threw for over 5,000 yards for the fourth time in his career, and Detroit Lions wide receiver Calvin Johnson, who set a new single-season record for receiving yards with 1,964.

Super Bowl XLVIII

Super Bowl XLVIII was played on February 2, 2014, at MetLife Stadium in East Rutherford, New Jersey. The game featured the Denver Broncos, representing the American Football Conference (AFC), and the Seattle Seahawks, representing the National Football Conference (NFC).

The game was highly anticipated, as it pitted the league's best offense, led by Broncos quarterback Peyton Manning, against the league's best defense, led by Seahawks cornerback Richard Sherman. However, the game turned out to be a lopsided affair, with the Seahawks dominating the Broncos from start to finish.

The Seahawks' defense set the tone early in the game, as linebacker Malcolm Smith intercepted a pass from Manning and returned it for a touchdown to give Seattle a 7-0 lead. From there, the Seahawks' defense continued to stifle the Broncos' offense, with the front seven applying constant pressure to Manning and the secondary locking down the Broncos' receivers.

On the other side of the ball, Seahawks' quarterback Russell Wilson played a mistake-free game, completing 18 of 25 passes for 206 yards and two touchdowns. Running back Marshawn Lynch also had a big game, rushing for 109 yards and a touchdown on 22 carries.

The game was essentially over by halftime, with the Seahawks leading 22-0. The Broncos were unable to mount a comeback in the second half, as the Seahawks' defense continued to dominate, and the offense added another touchdown to seal a 43-8 victory.

Malcolm Smith was named the game's Most Valuable Player, becoming the first defensive player to earn the honor since Tampa Bay Buccaneers' safety Dexter Jackson in Super Bowl XXXVII. Smith's interception return for a touchdown set the tone for the game and helped the Seahawks earn their first-ever Super Bowl victory.

Super Bowl XLVIII will be remembered as one of the most dominant defensive performances in Super Bowl history, as the Seahawks held the high-powered Broncos' offense to just eight points and 306 total yards. The victory cemented the Seahawks as one of the league's elite franchises and proved that defense can still win championships in the NFL.

The 2013 NFL season was an exciting one, filled with high-scoring games, intense rivalries, and thrilling playoff matchups. The Seattle Seahawks emerged as the top team in the league, winning their first Super Bowl in franchise history. The season also featured outstanding performances from several players, including Peyton Manning, Richard Sherman, and Marshawn Lynch. Overall, 2013 was a year of growth and change for the NFL, as the league continued to evolve to meet the changing needs of its fans and players.

2014

The NFL continued to be one of the most popular sports leagues in the world in 2014. The year saw the league making further efforts to improve player safety, as well as a number of exciting games, records broken, and controversies.

Player Safety

Player safety continued to be a top priority for the NFL in 2014. The league introduced a number of new rules and regulations aimed at reducing the risk of head injuries and concussions. One of the most significant changes was the introduction of a new protocol for managing head injuries during games. The protocol required any player who showed signs of a head injury to be immediately removed from the game and evaluated for a concussion.

The NFL also increased its penalties for players who committed helmet-to-helmet hits or other types of dangerous tackles. The league also made changes to the rules governing kickoffs, with the aim of reducing the number of high-speed collisions.

Records Broken

The 2014 season saw a number of records broken by individual players and teams. Quarterback Peyton Manning of the Denver Broncos broke the all-time record for career touchdown passes, previously held by Brett Favre. Manning finished the season with a total of 539 touchdown passes.

In addition, Dallas Cowboys running back DeMarco Murray broke the franchise record for rushing yards in a season, finishing the year with 1,845 yards. Murray also set an NFL record for the most consecutive games with 100 rushing yards, with a streak of eight games.

Exciting Games

The 2014 season saw a number of exciting games, with several matches going down to the wire. One of the most memorable games of the year was the NFC Championship Game between the Seattle Seahawks and the Green Bay Packers. The Seahawks trailed by 12 points with just over three minutes remaining, but scored two quick touchdowns to take the lead and win the game in overtime.

Another exciting game was the Thanksgiving Day matchup between the Dallas Cowboys and the Philadelphia Eagles. The Cowboys trailed by 21 points in the second half, but mounted a comeback to win the game in dramatic fashion.

Super Bowl XLIX

Super Bowl XLIX was the 49th edition of the Super Bowl, the championship game of the 2014 season. The game was played on February 1, 2015, at University of Phoenix Stadium in Glendale, Arizona.

The New England Patriots represented the American Football Conference (AFC) while the Seattle Seahawks represented the National Football Conference (NFC). The Patriots had a 12-4 record in the regular season and had defeated the Baltimore Ravens and the Indianapolis Colts in the playoffs to reach the Super Bowl. The Seahawks had a 12-4 record in the regular season and had defeated the Carolina Panthers and the Green Bay Packers in the playoffs to reach the Super Bowl.

The game was highly anticipated as both teams were considered to be evenly matched. The Patriots were led by quarterback Tom Brady, who had won three Super Bowls in his career. The Seahawks, on the other hand, were known for their dominant defense, which had allowed the fewest points in the league that season.

The game started off with a slow pace, with both teams struggling to move the ball. The first quarter ended with no points scored by either team. The Seahawks took the lead in the second quarter with a touchdown pass from quarterback Russell Wilson to wide receiver Chris Matthews. The Patriots responded with a touchdown of their own, a pass from Brady to wide receiver Brandon LaFell, to tie the game.

The Seahawks regained the lead in the third quarter with a touchdown run by running back Marshawn Lynch. The Patriots responded with two touchdowns in the fourth quarter, one on a pass from Brady to tight end Rob Gronkowski, and another on a touchdown run by running back James White. The Seahawks scored a touchdown with just over two minutes remaining in the game, but failed to convert on a two-point conversion, leaving the score at 28-24 in favor of the Patriots.

The Patriots were able to hold on for the win, securing their fourth Super Bowl championship in franchise history. Brady was named the game's Most Valuable Player (MVP) after throwing for 328 yards and four touchdowns. The game was also notable for its controversial ending, with the Seahawks choosing to pass the ball from the one-yard line instead of running it with Lynch, which resulted in an interception by the Patriots' Malcolm Butler to seal the victory.

Overall, Super Bowl XLIX was an exciting and dramatic game, showcasing the talent and skill of both teams. It was also a reminder of the importance of strategy and decision-making in football, as the Seahawks' controversial decision to pass the ball instead of running it ultimately cost them the game.

Controversies

The 2014 season was not without its controversies. One of the most significant was the Ray Rice scandal. Rice, a former running back for the Baltimore Ravens, was caught on video punching his then-fiancée in an elevator. The video went viral, and Rice was suspended indefinitely by the NFL. The scandal prompted widespread debate about domestic violence in the NFL and the league's handling of the issue.

The 2014 NFL season was a memorable one, with records broken, exciting games, and significant developments in player safety. While the league made progress in addressing head injuries and concussions, the Ray Rice scandal highlighted the need for further progress in addressing domestic violence and other social issues. Nevertheless, the 2014 season was a reminder of why the NFL continues to be one of the most popular sports leagues in the world, with millions of fans tuning in each week to watch their favorite teams and players in action.

The NFL continued to be one of the most popular sports leagues in the world in 2015. The year saw a number of exciting games, records broken, controversies, and significant developments in player safety.

Player Safety

Player safety remained a top priority for the NFL in 2015. The league continued to enforce stricter penalties for players who committed dangerous tackles or other types of illegal hits. The league also introduced new rules aimed at reducing the risk of head injuries and concussions, including changes to the kickoff rules and stricter enforcement of the rules governing helmet-to-helmet hits.

In addition, the NFL continued to invest in research and development of new equipment and technology aimed at improving player safety. The league also established a new partnership with the U.S. military to study the effects of concussions on service members.

Records Broken

The 2015 season saw a number of records broken by individual players and teams. Quarterback Drew Brees of the New Orleans Saints broke the record for most career passing yards, previously held by Peyton Manning. Brees finished the season with a total of 79,204 passing yards.

In addition, Carolina Panthers quarterback Cam Newton broke the record for most rushing touchdowns in a season by a quarterback, finishing the year with 14 touchdowns on the ground.

Exciting Games

The 2015 season saw a number of exciting games, with several matches going down to the wire. One of the most memorable games of the year was the NFC Divisional Round matchup between the Green Bay Packers and the Arizona Cardinals. The game went into overtime, with the Cardinals ultimately winning on a 5-yard touchdown pass from quarterback Carson Palmer to wide receiver Larry Fitzgerald.

Another exciting game was the Week 12 matchup between the Denver Broncos and the New England Patriots. The game was a highly anticipated rematch of the previous year's AFC Championship Game, with the Broncos winning in overtime on a touchdown pass from quarterback Brock Osweiler to tight end Virgil Green.

Super Bowl 50

Super Bowl 50, held on February 7, 2016, at Levi's Stadium in Santa Clara, California, was a historic event for the National Football League (NFL). The game featured the Denver Broncos, led by future Hall of Fame quarterback Peyton Manning, and the Carolina Panthers, led by the league's Most Valuable Player that season, quarterback Cam Newton.

The Broncos, known for their dominant defense, came out strong and took control of the game early. On the Panthers' first offensive possession, Broncos linebacker Von Miller forced a fumble by Newton that was recovered by defensive end Malik Jackson in the end zone for a touchdown. The Broncos defense continued to dominate throughout the game, sacking Newton six times and intercepting him once.

Despite the Broncos' strong defensive performance, the game remained close until the fourth quarter. With just over ten minutes remaining, Manning led the Broncos on a 13-play, 75-yard touchdown drive that culminated in a 4-yard touchdown pass to wide receiver Bennie Fowler. The Broncos defense continued to hold strong, and the game ended with a final score of 24-10 in favor of the Broncos.

The victory was particularly significant for Manning, who became the oldest quarterback to win a Super Bowl at age 39. It was also the second Super Bowl win of Manning's career, having previously won with the Indianapolis Colts in 2007.

For the Broncos, the win was their third Super Bowl victory in team history and their first since 1999. The team's dominant defense, led by Miller, was a key factor in their victory, and Miller was named the game's Most Valuable Player.

Super Bowl 50 also marked the end of an era for the NFL, as Manning announced his retirement from the game just weeks after the victory. His retirement was a bittersweet moment for fans, who had enjoyed watching one of the greatest quarterbacks of all time play for nearly two decades.

Overall, Super Bowl 50 was a memorable event for the NFL and its fans. It showcased the importance of a dominant defense in the modern game, and it provided a fitting end to the career of one of the league's greatest players.

Controversies

The 2015 season was not without its controversies. One of the most significant was the Deflategate scandal, which centered around allegations that the New England Patriots had deflated footballs during the AFC Championship Game against the Indianapolis Colts the previous season. The scandal led to a lengthy investigation by the NFL, which resulted in a four-game suspension for Patriots quarterback Tom Brady.

The season also saw a number of controversies surrounding player conduct off the field, including domestic violence allegations against several players and a number of arrests for various offenses.

The 2015 NFL season was a memorable one, with records broken, exciting games, and significant developments in player safety. While the league made progress in addressing head injuries and concussions, the Deflategate scandal highlighted the need for further progress in maintaining the integrity of the game. Nevertheless, the 2015 season was a reminder of why the NFL continues to be one of the most popular sports leagues in the world, with millions of fans tuning in each week to watch their favorite teams and players in action.

2016

The NFL continued to be one of the most popular sports leagues in the world in 2016. The year saw a number of exciting games, records broken, controversies, and significant developments in player safety.

Player Safety

Player safety remained a top priority for the NFL in 2016. The league continued to enforce stricter penalties for players who committed dangerous tackles or other types of illegal hits. The league also introduced new rules aimed at reducing the risk of head injuries and concussions, including changes to the kickoff rules and stricter enforcement of the rules governing helmet-to-helmet hits.

In addition, the NFL continued to invest in research and development of new equipment and technology aimed at improving player safety. The league also established a new partnership with the U.S. military to study the effects of concussions on service members.

Records Broken

The 2016 season saw a number of records broken by individual players and teams. Dallas Cowboys rookie running back Ezekiel Elliott led the league in rushing with 1,631 yards, breaking the franchise's rookie rushing record. New England Patriots quarterback Tom Brady also set a number of records, including most career touchdown passes in the playoffs and most playoff wins by a quarterback.

Exciting Games

The 2016 season saw a number of exciting games, with several matches going down to the wire. One of the most memorable games of the year was the Week 11 matchup between the Dallas Cowboys and the Pittsburgh Steelers. The game featured a number of lead changes and ended with a last-second field goal by the Cowboys, giving them a 35-30 victory.

Super Bowl LI

Super Bowl LI, held on February 5, 2017, at NRG Stadium in Houston, Texas, was one of the most memorable Super Bowls in NFL history. The game featured the New England Patriots, led by quarterback Tom Brady, and the Atlanta Falcons, led by quarterback Matt Ryan.

The game started off with the Falcons dominating on both sides of the ball. Ryan threw three touchdown passes in the first half, and the Falcons defense held the Patriots to just three points. In the third quarter, the Falcons continued to build their lead, scoring another touchdown to make the score 28-3.

However, in the fourth quarter, the Patriots mounted a historic comeback. Brady led the team on a string of scoring drives, throwing two touchdown passes and running in for a third. The Patriots defense also stepped up, holding the Falcons scoreless for the entire second half and forcing a critical fumble late in the game.

With just over two minutes left in regulation, the Patriots tied the game at 28-28, sending the game to overtime. In the extra period, the Patriots won the coin toss and drove down the field to score the game-winning touchdown, securing a 34-28 victory and their fifth Super Bowl title in team history.

Brady, who threw for a Super Bowl-record 466 yards and two touchdowns, was named the game's Most Valuable Player. The victory was particularly significant for Brady, who had been suspended for the first four games of the season for his role in the "Deflategate" scandal.

Super Bowl LI also marked the end of an era for the Falcons, who came agonizingly close to winning their first Super Bowl title in franchise history. The loss was a bitter disappointment for the team and its fans, but it was a reminder of the unpredictability and excitement that makes the Super Bowl one of the most watched sporting events in the world.

Overall, Super Bowl LI was a thrilling and historic event for the NFL and its fans. It showcased the importance of resilience, determination, and teamwork in the modern game, and it provided a fitting end to a season that will be remembered for its exciting games, record-breaking performances, and dramatic moments.

Controversies

The 2016 season was not without its controversies. One of the most significant was the ongoing debate surrounding player protests during the national anthem. San Francisco 49ers quarterback Colin Kaepernick began protesting police brutality and racial inequality by kneeling during the anthem, sparking a nationwide conversation about free speech, patriotism, and racial justice.

The season also saw a number of controversies surrounding player conduct off the field, including domestic violence allegations against several players and a number of arrests for various offenses.

The 2016 NFL season was a memorable one, with records broken, exciting games, and significant developments in player safety. While the league made progress in addressing head injuries and concussions, the ongoing debate over player protests highlighted the need for further progress in addressing issues of social justice. Nevertheless, the 2016 season was a reminder of why the NFL continues to be one of the most popular sports leagues in the world, with millions of fans tuning in each week to watch their favorite teams and players in action.

2017

The NFL in the year 2017 was full of excitement and drama. From thrilling games to controversial off-field incidents, the league kept fans and pundits alike engaged throughout the season. In this chapter, we will examine the major highlights and lowlights of the NFL in 2017.

On-field Action

The 2017 NFL season began on September 7, 2017, with a game between the Kansas City Chiefs and the defending Super Bowl champions, the New England Patriots. The Chiefs pulled off a stunning upset, winning 42-27. This set the tone for an unpredictable season, with several upsets and surprises throughout.

The season was also marked by a high number of injuries to key players, including Aaron Rodgers, J.J. Watt, and Odell Beckham Jr. These injuries had a significant impact on the performance of their respective teams, and some even missed the entire season.

The regular season ended on December 31, 2017, with the New England Patriots and the Pittsburgh Steelers finishing with the best records in the league at 13-3. The playoffs began on January 6, 2018, and culminated in Super Bowl LII on February 4, 2018, between the New England Patriots and the Philadelphia Eagles.

Off-field Controversies

The 2017 NFL season was also marked by several off-field controversies that grabbed headlines and sparked debates among fans and analysts. The most notable of these controversies were the ongoing protests by players during the national anthem.

The protests, which began in 2016, were initially sparked by former San Francisco 49ers quarterback Colin Kaepernick, who kneeled during the national anthem to protest police brutality and racial inequality in America. In 2017, several other players joined the protest, and it became a hot-button issue for the league.

The NFL's handling of the protests was heavily criticized, with some fans boycotting games and some sponsors pulling out of advertising deals. The controversy also became a political issue, with President Donald Trump condemning the protests and calling for players who kneeled during the anthem to be fired.

Another major controversy was the suspension of Dallas Cowboys running back Ezekiel Elliott for six games following allegations of domestic violence. Elliott denied the allegations and fought the suspension in court, but ultimately served the full six-game ban.

Super Bowl LII

Super Bowl LII was played on February 4, 2018, at U.S. Bank Stadium in Minneapolis, Minnesota. The game featured the New England Patriots, representing the American Football Conference (AFC), and the Philadelphia Eagles, representing the National Football Conference (NFC).

The game was highly anticipated, as it pitted the Patriots, one of the most successful franchises in NFL history, against the Eagles, who were playing in their first Super Bowl since 2004. The game did not disappoint, as it turned out to be one of the most exciting and high-scoring Super Bowls in NFL history.

The Eagles got off to a strong start, with quarterback Nick Foles throwing a touchdown pass to wide receiver Alshon Jeffery to give Philadelphia an early 9-3 lead. However, the Patriots responded with a touchdown pass from quarterback Tom Brady to tight end Rob Gronkowski to take a 10-9 lead.

The game remained close throughout the first half, with both teams trading touchdowns and field goals. The Eagles went into halftime with a 22-12 lead, but the Patriots were still very much in the game.

In the second half, the Eagles continued to play aggressive and creative football, with Foles throwing a touchdown pass to running back Corey Clement and then catching a touchdown pass of his own on a trick play known as the "Philly Special." The Patriots responded with a touchdown pass to Gronkowski and a field goal, but the Eagles held on to their lead, with Foles throwing another touchdown pass to tight end Zach Ertz.

The Patriots had one last chance to tie the game in the fourth quarter, but their potential game-tying drive ended with a strip-sack of Brady by Eagles defensive end Brandon Graham. The Eagles recovered the fumble and added a field goal to take a 41-33 lead, which they held until the end of the game.

Nick Foles was named the game's Most Valuable Player, completing 28 of 43 passes for 373 yards and three touchdowns. The Eagles' defense also played a key role in the victory, sacking Brady three times and intercepting him once.

Super Bowl LII will be remembered as one of the most exciting and high-scoring Super Bowls in NFL history, with both teams combining for a record-breaking 1,151 yards of total offense. The victory was the first Super Bowl title in Eagles franchise history, and it cemented Nick Foles' place in NFL history as one of the greatest backup quarterbacks of all time.

Overall, the NFL in the year 2017 was full of ups and downs. On the field, there were thrilling games and surprising upsets, but injuries to key players had a significant impact on the season. Off the field, the league faced several controversies, including the ongoing protests during the national anthem and the suspension of Ezekiel Elliott. Despite these challenges, the NFL remained one of the most popular and watched sports leagues in America.

2018

The NFL in the year 2018 was another eventful year for the league. The 2018 NFL season saw some incredible on-field performances and dramatic moments, as well as significant off-field controversies that kept the league in the headlines. Let's examine the major highlights and lowlights of the NFL in 2018.

On-field Action

The 2018 NFL season began on September 6, 2018, with the defending Super Bowl champions, the Philadelphia Eagles, defeating the Atlanta Falcons 18-12 in the season opener. The regular season saw some incredible performances from teams and players, with several memorable games and moments.

The Los Angeles Rams emerged as one of the top teams in the league, finishing with a 13-3 record and securing the number one seed in the playoffs. The New England Patriots, led by Tom Brady, once again proved to be a formidable team, finishing with an 11-5 record and securing the number two seed in the playoffs.

Super Bowl LIII

Super Bowl LIII was the 53rd edition of the annual championship game of the NFL. The game was played on February 3, 2019, at Mercedes-Benz Stadium in Atlanta, Georgia, and was contested by the New England Patriots and the Los Angeles Rams.

The New England Patriots, led by quarterback Tom Brady and head coach Bill Belichick, were making their third consecutive Super Bowl appearance and their ninth in total, having won the championship five times previously. The Los Angeles Rams, led by head coach Sean McVay and quarterback Jared Goff, were appearing in their first Super Bowl since the 2001 season when they were based in St. Louis.

The game was a defensive battle, with both teams struggling to move the ball early on. The first quarter ended with no score, and the Patriots took a 3-0 lead early in the second quarter on a field goal by kicker Stephen Gostkowski. The Rams tied the game late in the second quarter with a field goal of their own, and the first half ended tied 3-3.

The third quarter was scoreless, and the game remained tied heading into the fourth quarter. The Patriots took a 10-3 lead early in the quarter on a touchdown run by Sony Michel, but the Rams responded with a field goal to cut the deficit to 10-6.

The Patriots put the game away with a touchdown pass from Brady to receiver Julian Edelman with just over seven minutes remaining in the game, giving them a 17-6 lead. The Rams had one final chance to mount a comeback, but Goff was intercepted by Patriots cornerback Stephon Gilmore with just over four minutes remaining, effectively ending the game.

The final score was 13-3 in favor of the New England Patriots, who won their sixth Super Bowl championship, tying the Pittsburgh Steelers for the most all-time. Patriots receiver Julian Edelman was named the game's Most Valuable Player, finishing with 10 catches for 141 yards.

The game was criticized by some fans and analysts for its lack of scoring and excitement, but it was still a historic moment for the Patriots and their fans. The victory cemented the legacies of Brady and Belichick as two of the greatest in NFL history and solidified the Patriots as one of the most successful franchises in sports.

Off-field Controversies

The 2018 NFL season was also marked by several off-field controversies that sparked debates and headlines throughout the year. The most notable of these controversies was the ongoing controversy surrounding players kneeling during the national anthem.

The protests, which began in 2016, were continued by several players in the 2018 season, but the controversy began to die down. The NFL introduced a new policy in May 2018 that required players to stand during the national anthem or remain in the locker room, but the policy was later put on hold due to objections from the players' union.

Another significant off-field controversy was the domestic violence allegations against former Kansas City Chiefs running back Kareem Hunt. Video footage surfaced in November 2018 showing Hunt assaulting a woman in a hotel hallway. The Chiefs released Hunt, and he was later signed by the Cleveland Browns.

The NFL in the year 2018 was another eventful year for the league, with some incredible on-field performances and dramatic moments. However, the league also faced significant off-field controversies, including the ongoing protests during the national anthem and the domestic violence allegations against Kareem Hunt. Despite these challenges, the NFL remained one of the most popular and watched sports leagues in America.

2019

The NFL in the year 2019 was another exciting year for the league. The 2019 NFL season saw some incredible on-field performances and dramatic moments, as well as significant off-field controversies that kept the league in the headlines. In this chapter, we will examine the major highlights and lowlights of the NFL in 2019.

On-field Action

The 2019 NFL season began on September 5, 2019, with the defending Super Bowl champions, the New England Patriots, defeating the Pittsburgh Steelers 33-3 in the season opener. The regular season saw some incredible performances from teams and players, with several memorable games and moments.

The Baltimore Ravens emerged as one of the top teams in the league, finishing with a 14-2 record and securing the number one seed in the playoffs. Quarterback Lamar Jackson had a breakout season, winning the league's Most Valuable Player (MVP) award. The Kansas City Chiefs, led by quarterback Patrick Mahomes, once again proved to be a formidable team, finishing with a 12-4 record and securing the number two seed in the playoffs.

Super Bowl LIV

Super Bowl LIV was the 54th edition of the annual championship game of the National Football League (NFL). The game was played on February 2, 2020, at Hard Rock Stadium in Miami Gardens, Florida, and was contested by the Kansas City Chiefs and the San Francisco 49ers.

The Kansas City Chiefs, led by quarterback Patrick Mahomes and head coach Andy Reid, were making their first Super Bowl appearance in 50 years. The San Francisco 49ers, led by head coach Kyle Shanahan and a dominant defense, were appearing in their first Super Bowl since the 2012 season.

The game started off as a defensive battle, with the 49ers taking an early 3-0 lead on a field goal by kicker Robbie Gould. The Chiefs responded with a touchdown pass from Mahomes to receiver Tyreek Hill, giving them a 7-3 lead. The 49ers regained the lead in the second quarter with a touchdown run by running back Raheem Mostert, but the Chiefs tied the game before halftime with a field goal by kicker Harrison Butker.

The third quarter was scoreless, and the game remained tied at 10-10 heading into the fourth quarter. The 49ers took the lead early in the fourth quarter with another touchdown run by Mostert, but the Chiefs responded with a touchdown pass from Mahomes to tight end Travis Kelce, tying the game at 20-20.

With just over six minutes remaining in the game, Mahomes led the Chiefs on a crucial drive that ended with a touchdown pass to running back Damien Williams, giving the Chiefs a 27-20 lead. The 49ers had one final chance to mount a comeback, but quarterback Jimmy Garoppolo was intercepted by Chiefs cornerback Kendall Fuller, effectively ending the game.

The final score was 31-20 in favor of the Kansas City Chiefs, who won their second Super Bowl championship and their first in 50 years. Mahomes was named the game's Most Valuable Player, finishing with 286 passing yards, two touchdown passes, and one rushing touchdown.

The game was praised by fans and analysts for its exciting back-and-forth action and the heroics of Mahomes and the Chiefs. The victory cemented Mahomes' status as one of the top quarterbacks in the league and solidified the Chiefs as one of the premier franchises in the NFL.

Off-field Controversies

The 2019 NFL season was also marked by several off-field controversies that sparked debates and headlines throughout the year. The most notable of these controversies was the ongoing controversy surrounding Colin Kaepernick and his protests during the national anthem.

Kaepernick had not played in the NFL since the 2016 season, when he began kneeling during the national anthem to protest police brutality and racial inequality. In November 2019, the NFL organized a workout for Kaepernick to showcase his skills to NFL teams, but the workout was ultimately moved to a different location after Kaepernick disagreed with the terms of the workout. Kaepernick remained unsigned by an NFL team at the end of the season.

Another significant off-field controversy was the domestic violence allegations against former Cleveland Browns defensive end Myles Garrett. During a game in November 2019, Garrett ripped off the helmet of Pittsburgh Steelers quarterback Mason Rudolph and hit him over the head with it. Garrett was suspended indefinitely by the NFL, but his suspension was eventually reduced to six games.

The NFL in the year 2019 was another eventful year for the league, with some incredible on-field performances and dramatic moments. However, the league also faced significant off-field controversies, including the ongoing controversy surrounding Colin Kaepernick and the domestic violence allegations against Myles Garrett. Despite these challenges, the NFL remained one of the most popular and watched sports leagues in America.

THE 2020'S

2020 – A global pandemic

The year 2020 was a challenging year for the NFL due to the COVID-19 pandemic. The league had to adapt quickly to the changing circumstances to ensure the safety of players, coaches, and fans while still maintaining the high level of competition and excitement that fans have come to expect.

COVID-19 and the NFL

The COVID-19 pandemic had a significant impact on the NFL in 2020. The league was forced to make several adjustments to the schedule, including canceling preseason games and implementing strict protocols to protect the health and safety of players, coaches, and staff.

Despite these challenges, the NFL was able to complete a full regular season and playoffs. The league also allowed a limited number of fans to attend games, with each team having its own guidelines for capacity and safety protocols.

On-field Action

The on-field action in the 2020 NFL season was as exciting and competitive as ever, with several teams and players delivering standout performances.

The Kansas City Chiefs, led by quarterback Patrick Mahomes, continued to dominate the league, finishing with a 14-2 record and securing the number one seed in the playoffs. The Pittsburgh Steelers and the Buffalo Bills also had strong seasons, finishing with 12-4 records and securing the number two and three seeds, respectively.

Super Bowl LV

Super Bowl LV, also known as Super Bowl 55, was the championship game of the National Football League (NFL) for the 2020 season. The game was played on February 7, 2021, at Raymond James Stadium in Tampa, Florida. The game featured the American Football Conference (AFC) champion Kansas City Chiefs and the National Football Conference (NFC) champion Tampa Bay Buccaneers. The Buccaneers won the game 31-9, marking their second Super Bowl victory in franchise history and the first Super Bowl played in a team's home stadium.

The lead-up to Super Bowl LV was dominated by the matchup between two of the greatest quarterbacks in NFL history: the Chiefs' Patrick Mahomes and the Buccaneers' Tom Brady. Mahomes was the reigning Super Bowl MVP and had led the Chiefs to a 14-2 regular-season record and victories over the Cleveland Browns and the Buffalo Bills in the playoffs. Brady, meanwhile, was making his tenth Super Bowl appearance and had led the Buccaneers to an 11-5 regular-season record and victories over the Washington Football Team, the New Orleans Saints, and the Green Bay Packers in the playoffs.

The game was also notable for the matchup between the Chiefs' high-powered offense, which had led the league in scoring during the regular season, and the Buccaneers' dominant defense, which had recorded the second-most sacks and forced the most turnovers in the league.

The Buccaneers got off to a fast start, scoring on their first two possessions to take a 14-3 lead. Brady threw touchdown passes to Rob Gronkowski and Antonio Brown in the first quarter, and Leonard Fournette added a touchdown run in the second quarter to extend the lead to 21-6 at halftime.

The Chiefs struggled to get their offense going, with Mahomes under constant pressure from the Buccaneers' pass rush. Mahomes was sacked three times in the first half and completed just nine of 19 passes for 67 yards. The Chiefs' only points in the first half came on field goals by Harrison Butker.

The Buccaneers continued to dominate in the second half, with Fournette adding another touchdown run in the third quarter to make it 28-9. The Chiefs had a chance to get back in the game early in the fourth quarter, but a fourth-down pass by Mahomes was dropped by receiver Tyreek Hill in the end zone.

The Buccaneers added a field goal late in the fourth quarter to make the final score 31-9. Brady was named the game's Most Valuable Player, completing 21 of 29 passes for 201 yards and three touchdowns. Fournette rushed for 89 yards and a touchdown on 16 carries, while Gronkowski caught six passes for 67 yards and two touchdowns.

The Buccaneers' victory in Super Bowl LV was a historic achievement, as they became the first team in NFL history to win a Super Bowl in their home stadium. It was also Brady's seventh Super Bowl victory, extending his record for the most championships by a player in NFL history.

The game was a disappointing performance for the Chiefs, who had been considered the favorites to win heading into the game. Mahomes, who had been battling a toe injury, was unable to overcome the Buccaneers' fierce pass rush and struggled to connect with his receivers. The Chiefs' defense, which had been criticized for much of the season, was also unable to slow down the Buccaneers' offense.

Off-field Controversies

The 2020 NFL season was also marked by several off-field controversies that sparked debates and headlines throughout the year. The most notable of these controversies was the ongoing controversy surrounding social justice issues and player protests during the national anthem.

Several players and coaches took a knee during the national anthem to protest police brutality and racial inequality. The league also launched several initiatives to promote social justice, including the NFL's Inspire Change program and the league's donation of $250 million over 10 years to support social justice causes.

Another significant off-field controversy was the sexual harassment and workplace misconduct allegations against the Washington Football Team. An investigation by the league found that the team had engaged in a pattern of harassment and misconduct, leading to the resignation of team owner Dan Snyder's wife and several high-level executives.

The NFL in the year 2020 faced significant challenges due to the COVID-19 pandemic, but the league was able to adapt and complete a successful season. The on-field action was as competitive and exciting as ever, with the Kansas City Chiefs and Tampa Bay Buccaneers emerging as the top teams in the league. The NFL also faced significant off-field controversies, including the ongoing debate over social justice issues and the sexual harassment and misconduct allegations against the Washington Football Team. Despite these challenges, the NFL remained one of the most popular and watched sports leagues in America.

2021

The NFL in the year 2021 was a season of excitement, drama, and unexpected twists. The COVID-19 pandemic continued to impact the league, with protocols in place to ensure the safety of players, coaches, and fans. Despite the challenges, the 2021 NFL season was filled with memorable moments and highlights.

COVID-19 and the NFL

The COVID-19 pandemic continued to impact the NFL in the 2021 season. The league implemented strict protocols to protect the health and safety of players, coaches, and staff. Vaccination was encouraged but not mandated, and some players faced repercussions for refusing to get vaccinated.

The NFL allowed fans to attend games, but each team had its own guidelines for capacity and safety protocols. The league also allowed for flexible scheduling to account for any games that may need to be postponed due to COVID-19 outbreaks.

On-field Action

The on-field action in the 2021 NFL season was filled with drama, excitement, and unexpected twists. The Tampa Bay Buccaneers, the reigning Super Bowl champions, struggled early in the season but found their stride in the second half of the season, finishing with a 13-4 record and securing the number two seed in the playoffs.

The Green Bay Packers had another strong season, finishing with a 13-4 record and securing the number one seed in the playoffs. The Dallas Cowboys and the Los Angeles Rams also had strong seasons, finishing with 12-5 records and securing the number three and four seeds, respectively.

Super Bowl LVI

Super Bowl LVI was the culmination of the 2021 NFL
season and took place on February 13, 2022, at SoFi
Stadium in Inglewood, California. The game featured the
AFC champion Cincinnati Bengals and the NFC champion
Los Angeles Rams.

The Bengals, led by quarterback Joe Burrow, were looking
for their first Super Bowl win in franchise history. The
Rams, led by quarterback Matthew Stafford, were seeking
their second Super Bowl championship and first since
moving to Los Angeles.

The game got off to a slow start, with both teams struggling
to score in the first quarter. The Bengals struck first in the
second quarter with a touchdown pass from Burrow to
Tyler Boyd, but the Rams responded with a touchdown run
by Cam Akers.

The Bengals added a field goal before halftime to take a
10-7 lead into the break. The Rams tied the game early in
the third quarter with a field goal, but the Bengals regained
the lead with another touchdown pass from Burrow to
Boyd.

The Rams responded with a touchdown pass from Stafford
to Van Jefferson to tie the game once again. The Bengals
took the lead once again with a field goal, but the Rams
answered with a field goal of their own to tie the game at
20-20.

In the fourth quarter, the Rams took the lead with a
touchdown pass from Stafford to Cooper Kupp, who had a
standout game with 10 receptions for 145 yards and the
game-winning touchdown. The Bengals had a chance to tie

the game late in the fourth quarter but were unable to convert on fourth down, sealing the Rams' victory.

The final score was 23-20 in favor of the Rams, who won their second Super Bowl championship in franchise history. Stafford was named the game's Most Valuable Player, completing 25 of 32 passes for 302 yards and one touchdown.

The game was a thrilling conclusion to the 2021 NFL season, and it cemented the Rams as one of the league's top teams. For the Bengals, the loss was disappointing but provided a glimpse of a bright future led by the talented Burrow.

Off-field Controversies

The 2021 NFL season was also marked by several off-field controversies that sparked debates and headlines throughout the year. The most notable of these controversies was the ongoing debate over player protests during the national anthem and the league's handling of the issue.

Another significant off-field controversy was the sexual harassment and workplace misconduct allegations against the Las Vegas Raiders. An investigation by the league found that the team had engaged in a pattern of harassment and misconduct, leading to the resignation of several high-level executives, including head coach Jon Gruden.

The NFL also faced scrutiny over its handling of player conduct issues, including domestic violence and sexual assault allegations. The league implemented new policies to address these issues, including stronger penalties for players found guilty of these offenses.

The NFL in the year 2021 was a season of excitement, drama, and unexpected twists. The league continued to navigate the challenges posed by the COVID-19 pandemic, implementing strict protocols to protect the health and safety of players, coaches, and staff. The on-field action was filled with standout performances from top teams and players, culminating in an exciting Super Bowl between the Los Angeles Rams and the Cincinnati Bengals. The league also faced several off-field controversies, highlighting the need for continued efforts to address social justice issues and player conduct issues. Despite these challenges, the NFL remained one of the most popular and watched sports leagues in America.

2022

In 2022, the NFL continued to be a dominant force in the sports world, with new innovations and challenges that marked its ongoing evolution.

The State of the NFL in 2022

In 2022, the NFL continued to face challenges related to player health and safety, COVID-19, as well as concerns about declining TV ratings and fan engagement. However, the league remained focused on finding innovative solutions to these challenges, including new technology, rule changes, and outreach initiatives.

One significant development in 2022 was the continued expansion of the NFL's international presence. The league had already made significant strides in this area in recent years, with the addition of international games in London and Mexico City, as well as the establishment of an NFL China office. In 2022, the NFL announced plans to expand its international presence even further, with the addition of new games in Europe, Asia, and other regions.

Another major trend in 2022 was the growing importance of player activism and social justice issues. This was exemplified by the ongoing controversy over the league's handling of player protests during the national anthem. However, the NFL also took steps to support player activism, including the establishment of a new social justice fund and the expansion of its My Cause, My Cleats program.

Top Players in 2022

In 2022, the NFL featured many of the same elite players that had dominated the league in previous years, including quarterbacks such as Tom Brady, Patrick Mahomes, and Aaron Rodgers. However, there were also several up-and-coming stars who emerged as major forces in the league.

One of the most notable of these players was Lamar Jackson, quarterback for the Baltimore Ravens. Jackson had already established himself as one of the most dynamic and exciting players in the league, with his ability to run the ball and make big plays with his arm. In 2022, Jackson continued to improve his passing accuracy and led the Ravens to a division title.

Another standout player in 2022 was Aaron Donald, defensive tackle for the Los Angeles Rams. Donald had long been recognized as one of the best defensive players in the league, but in 2022 he took his game to another level. He led the league in sacks and tackles for loss, earning him his third Defensive Player of the Year award.

In addition to these established stars, there were also several rookies who made an immediate impact in 2022. One of the most notable of these was Trevor Lawrence, quarterback for the Jacksonville Jaguars. Lawrence had been touted as a generational talent coming out of college, and he did not disappoint in his rookie season, leading the Jaguars to their first playoff appearance in over a decade.

Super Bowl LVII

Super Bowl LVII, also known as Super Bowl 57, was held on February 5th, 2023, at Allegiant Stadium in Las Vegas, Nevada. The Super Bowl is the annual championship game of the National Football League (NFL) and is one of the most-watched television events in the world.

The teams that competed in Super Bowl LVII were the Kansas City Chiefs and the Los Angeles Rams. The Chiefs, led by quarterback Patrick Mahomes, were looking to win their second Super Bowl in three years. The Rams, led by quarterback Matthew Stafford, were looking to win their first Super Bowl since moving to Los Angeles in 2016.

The game was highly anticipated, as both teams had high-powered offenses and strong defenses. The first half of the game was a back-and-forth battle, with each team scoring two touchdowns. The Chiefs took an early lead with a touchdown pass from Mahomes to wide receiver Tyreek Hill, but the Rams responded with a touchdown pass from Stafford to tight end Tyler Higbee.

In the second half, the Chiefs pulled ahead with another touchdown pass from Mahomes to Hill, followed by a rushing touchdown by running back Clyde Edwards-Helaire. The Rams tried to mount a comeback, but were unable to overcome the deficit. The Chiefs ultimately won the game with a final score of 28-17.

Mahomes was named the Super Bowl MVP for the second time in three years, having completed 27 of 36 passes for 345 yards and two touchdowns. Hill was also a standout performer, catching 10 passes for 135 yards and two touchdowns. On the defensive side of the ball, Chiefs linebacker Willie Gay Jr. had a strong performance, recording nine tackles, two sacks, and an interception.

For the Rams, Stafford completed 28 of 40 passes for 304 yards and two touchdowns, but was also intercepted twice. Wide receiver Cooper Kupp had a solid performance, catching nine passes for 118 yards and a touchdown. On defense, Rams defensive tackle Aaron Donald had a dominant performance, recording three sacks and four tackles for loss.

Super Bowl LVII was a significant event for the NFL, as it showcased two of the league's top teams and most exciting players. The game was also notable for being held in Las Vegas, which had recently become the home of the Raiders after the team relocated from Oakland.

The game had a significant impact on the legacy of Mahomes, who had already established himself as one of the top quarterbacks in the league. With his second Super Bowl victory and MVP award, Mahomes solidified his place among the all-time greats of the game.

The game also had an impact on the future of the NFL, as it highlighted the importance of strong offenses and dynamic quarterbacks in today's game. The NFL is likely to continue to focus on promoting high-scoring and exciting games in order to maintain its position as one of the top sports leagues in the world.

Super Bowl LVII was a thrilling game that showcased the best of the NFL. With its high-powered offenses, strong defenses, and standout performances by some of the league's top players, the game was a fitting conclusion to the 2022 NFL season. As the NFL continues to evolve and adapt to new challenges, it is clear that the Super Bowl will remain a highlight of the sports calendar for years to come.

Innovations and Changes in 2022

The NFL continued to explore new technologies and rule changes in 2022, with the goal of improving player safety and enhancing the fan experience. One major innovation in 2022 was the expanded use of virtual and augmented reality technology, which allowed fans to experience games in a more immersive and interactive way.

The league also implemented several rule changes aimed at reducing player injuries and improving the pace of the game. One of the most significant of these changes was the adoption of a new helmet rule, which required players to wear helmets that met specific safety standards. The league also experimented with a new format for overtime games, which allowed both teams to have a possession regardless of the outcome of the first possession.

In 2022, the NFL continued to face challenges and evolve in new and exciting ways. From expanding its international presence to supporting player activism and exploring new technologies and rules.

THE FUTURE OF THE NFL

The National Football League has been a staple of American sports for over a century, and it continues to captivate audiences around the world. As the league enters a new era, there are a number of factors that will shape the future of the NFL.

The Impact of Technology

Technology has already had a significant impact on the NFL, with advances in areas such as player tracking and virtual reality changing the way that the game is played and experienced. In the future, we can expect technology to continue to play a major role in the NFL, with the league exploring new ways to engage fans and improve player safety through the use of technology.

The Changing Fan Experience

The fan experience has always been an important part of the NFL, and in the future, we can expect this to become even more important. With the rise of social media and digital media, the NFL will need to continue to adapt and evolve to provide fans with the best possible experience. This may include new ways to engage with fans, such as interactive fan experiences and augmented reality broadcasts.

The Future of Player Safety

Player safety has been a major concern for the NFL in recent years, and this trend is likely to continue in the future. The league will need to continue to invest in new technologies and strategies to improve player safety, while also ensuring that the game remains exciting and entertaining for fans.

The Globalization of the NFL

The NFL has already made significant strides in expanding its reach beyond the United States, with games being played in London and Mexico City in recent years. In the future, we can expect the NFL to continue to expand globally, as the league looks to tap into new markets and reach new fans around the world.

The Evolution of the Game

The game of football has evolved significantly over the years, and in the future, we can expect it to continue to evolve. This may include changes to the rules of the game, new strategies and tactics, and new technologies that change the way the game is played.

The Future of Ownership

The ownership structure of the NFL is likely to evolve in the future, as new investors and technologies emerge. This may include the rise of fan-owned teams, or the use of block chain technology to revolutionize the way that teams are owned and managed.

As the NFL enters a new era, it will need to continue to adapt and evolve to stay relevant and exciting for fans around the world. With the help of new technologies, new strategies for player safety, and a continued focus on the fan experience, the NFL has a bright future ahead of it.

CONCLUSION

The National Football League has come a long way since its humble beginnings in 1920. From its early days as a small league made up of just a few teams, to its current status as a multi-billion dollar industry with a worldwide following, the NFL has undergone numerous changes and transformations throughout its history.

Throughout this book, we have explored the many milestones, triumphs, controversies, and challenges that have shaped the NFL over the past century. From the early pioneers of the game to the modern-day superstars, we have witnessed the incredible feats of some of the most talented athletes in the world, as well as the rise and fall of some of the league's most iconic teams.

We have also seen how the league has evolved in response to social and cultural changes, as well as the impact of technology on the game of football. While the NFL has faced many challenges over the years, from labor disputes to controversies over player safety and concussions, the league has remained steadfast in its commitment to the game and to its fans.

As we look to the future of the NFL, it is clear that the league will continue to evolve and change, adapting to new technologies and new challenges as they arise. But no matter what the future holds, one thing is certain: the NFL will remain a beloved institution, a symbol of American sports and culture, and a source of inspiration and excitement for millions of fans around the world.

Thank You

Writing this book would not have been possible without the help and support of many people. First and foremost, I would like to thank the NFL itself, for providing such a rich and fascinating history to explore. I would also like to thank the many journalists, historians, and researchers who have documented the league's history over the years, and whose work has been invaluable in the writing of this book.

I would like to thank my editor for their guidance and support throughout the writing process, as well as my friends and family for their encouragement and inspiration.

And finally, I would like to thank you, the reader, for your interest in the history of the NFL. I hope that this book has provided you with a deeper appreciation and understanding of one of the greatest sports leagues in the world!

OTHER BOOKS BY JAMES BREN

The History of MMA

Printed in Great Britain
by Amazon